Indian Slavery
in Colonial Times
Within the Present Limits
of the United States
(1913)

Almon Wheeler Lauber
(1880-1944)

Originally published
1913

Contents

PREFACE...V

PART I. THE INSTITUTION AS PRACTICED BY THE INDIANS,
THE SPANIARDS AND THE FRENCH 1

CHAPTER I. ENSLAVEMENT BY THE INDIANS THEMSELVES..1

CHAPTER II. ENSLAVEMENT BY THE SPANIARDS....................13

CHAPTER III. ENSLAVEMENT BY THE FRENCH.........................23

PART II. THE INSTITUTION AS PRACTICED BY THE ENGLISH ...47

CHAPTER IV. THE NUMBER OF INDIAN SLAVES.......................47

CHAPTER V. PROCESSES OF ENSLAVEMENT: WARFARE 53

CHAPTER VI. PROCESSES OF ENSLAVEMENT: KIDNAPPING .73

CHAPTER VII. PROCESSES OF ENSLAVEMENT: TRADE...........81

CHAPTER VIII. OTHER PROCESSES of ENSLAVEMENT 99

CHAPTER IX. PROPERTY RELATIONS 109

CHAPTER X. METHODS OF EMPLOYMENT 127

CHAPTER XI. TREATMENT...133

CHAPTER XII. THE DECLINE OF INDIAN SLAVERY 153

PREFACE

It is the purpose of this study to bring to light a hitherto neglected phase of early American history: the enslavement of the Indians. The extensiveness of negro slavery in comparison with Indian slavery has so emphasized the former that, in the study of the institution in general, the existence of Indian slavery during the colonial period has almost entirely been lost sight of. In this discussion it is shown that the enslavement of the natives was practiced by the Indians themselves, the Spanish, the French and the English; yet in the case of no one of the European nations did it exist as a system separate and distinct from negro slavery. Though the holding of Indians as slaves by three of the European nations has been considered, it is the author's intention to lay emphasis chiefly upon the institution as practiced by the English.

The fact that hitherto no special attention has been given to the subject of Indian slavery has made the gathering of material difficult. Many of the important sources treating of the subject have never been published and are widely scattered. Much of even this material is vague in nature and consequently more or less unsatisfactory. The rapid increase in the number of negro slaves during the colonial period resulted in the general use of such terms as "slaves, negroes and other slaves and negroes," without specification of Indian slaves as such. This is true particularly of the colonial laws, even in the case of those colonies where Indian slavery existed to the greatest extent.

The author desires to express his indebtedness to Mrs. N. M. Surrey for her generous permission to use manuscript material collected in the southern states; to the librarians and their assistants of the Massachusetts Historical Society, the New York Historical Society, the Pennsylvania Historical Society, and the Maryland Historical Society, for their many kindnesses; and to Professor Herbert L. Osgood, of Columbia University, for his advice and for the use of extracts from the records of the Society for the Propagation of the Gospel in Foreign Parts. The author's most sincere thanks are due to Professor William R. Shepherd, of Columbia University, under whose guidance this work has been carried on. His suggestions and criticisms have been invaluable, and he has given unsparingly of his time in reading both manuscript and proof.

v

ALMON W. LAUBER. New York CITY, MARCH 15, 1913.

PART I. THE INSTITUTION AS PRACTICED BY THE INDIANS, THE SPANIARDS AND THE FRENCH

CHAPTER I. ENSLAVEMENT BY THE INDIANS THEMSELVES

THE discussion of the use of Indians as slaves by the aborigines within the present limits of the United States, both before and after the coming of the Europeans, may be prefaced by the statement that the institution of slavery in some form was practically universal. Certain tribes held slaves more generally than others, and various tribes were more subject to enslavement than others, according to their relative strength and weakness. Yet nowhere in the territory under discussion did slavery exist on such an extensive scale that some tribes held others in a state of subjection and demanded servile labor from them.

Slavery among the tribes of the Great Plains and the Atlantic Slope was different in nature from that in the northwest. Frequent mention of such slavery is found, but it has been shown that the term "slave" was often used by the early Spanish and French writers in an erroneous sense as synonymous with "prisoner." The institution of adoption so largely used by the American Indians, and incident to intertribal warfare and the consequent depletion of the tribal numbers, has also been confused by the writers with the institution of slavery.

Though slavery, in the strictest sense, was not general in the territory above mentioned, yet some form of the institution is recorded as having existed among the leading tribes. In the discussion which follows, the term "slave" must, then, be considered in its broadest sense. A prisoner held by his captor as an inferior and forced to labor for him, or sold into servitude or freedom for the financial benefit of his captor, will be considered a slave when thus treated by the Indians, as he will be so considered in a later discussion when thus treated by the whites.

Among the Aztec Indians of Mexico outcasts and criminals of the tribe were enslaved, and the usage appears to have been followed,

1

to a very slight extent, by Indians in the area of the French and English colonies to the northward.

Individual instances of slavery proceeded from other causes. The Indians were inveterate gamblers, and when nothing else was left, both men and women not infrequently staked themselves to serve as slaves in case of loss. Such slavery was sometimes for life, and sometimes for such short periods of time as a year or two. In case of famine, the Indians even sold their children to obtain food.

The slaves possessed by a given Indian tribe were oftener obtained through barter with other tribes. This intertribal traffic, though probably not common, was evidently farreaching. Owing to the wandering habits of the Indians and their custom of bartering goods with other tribes, articles of copper became distributed throughout the Northwest, especially in Wisconsin. The Illinois Indians possessed slaves who came from the sea coast, probably Florida. The Illinois also bartered their slaves with the Ottawa for guns, powder, kettles and knives, and with the Iroquois to obtain peace. Marquette found (1673) among the Arkansas Indians, knives, beads and hatchets which had been obtained partly from the Illinois and partly from the Indians farther to the east. The Jesuit, Grelon, relates that in Chinese Tartary he met a Huron woman whom he had known in America.

The transition from the method of obtaining slaves by actual warfare and barter to that of mere slave raids was an easy one. The desire to gain the reputation of a skillful hunter, and, still more, of a brave warrior, and thus to win the esteem and regard of his tribesmen, was inherent among the natives. To be a brave warrior was to be truly a man. So eager was the Indian to acquire the name of "brave" that he unhesitatingly underwent any hardships to obtain slaves or scalps as a proof of his qualifications for the title. This means of obtaining slaves was used by the stronger tribes like the Illinois and the Iroquois.

The slaves bartered by the Illinois were generally taken in the territory beyond the Mississippi. This the Illinois were better able to do after the coming of the whites, as they were provided with guns, while the Indians to the westward had no weapons of the sort. One of the chief sources from which these slaves was obtained was the

Pawnee nation. In 1719, Du Tisné wrote to Bienville, the commandant at New Orleans, that the Pawnee were afraid of him when he arrived among them, as their neighbors, the Osage, had made them believe that his intention was to entrap and enslave them.

The same practice was followed by the other northern tribes. La Jeune, in 1632, found slaves among the Algonquin. The Indians of the Great Lakes region had a young Esquimaux as a slave in 1646. Tonti found Iroquois slaves among the Huron and Ottawa. The Dutch navigator, Hendrickson, in 1616, found the Indians of the Schuylkill River country holding Indian slaves.

Of all the northern Indians, the Iroquois were by far the most powerful. They were the enemies, in the time of the early French explorations and settlements, of the Huron and the Illinois, and from these tribes they took many captives whom they enslaved. The statement has been made that no personal slavery ever existed among the Iroquois—that their captives were either killed or adopted as a part of the nation. Quite the contrary is true. They held both Indians and whites in personal slavery. They brought back from the Ohio country bands of captives, sometimes numbering three or four hundred. They preyed upon the Shawnee and carried them off into slavery. They captured and enslaved the Miami for whose redemption they were presented with quantities of beaver skin. These they received but failed to free the slaves. They brought home slaves from Maryland and the south, and from the land of the "Chat" (the Erie). It was the Iroquois (the Seneca), called by an early writer "Sonnagars," who enslaved captives taken from the tribes of Carolina and Florida.

Similar practices are related of the southern Indians. The Virginia tribes possessed "people of a rank inferior to the commons, a sort of servants . . . called black boys, attendant upon the gentry." When Menendez founded St. Augustine in 1565, he discovered in a native village the descendants of a band of Cuban Indians who had come to the mainland, been taken prisoners by the Florida Indians, and reduced to slavery.

In the south the strongest tribes were the Choctaw and Chickasaw. These two tribes were not only at war with each other from time to time, but each preyed upon the weaker tribes of the surrounding country. In 1717, a Cadodaquiou chief informed La

3

Harpe, on his journey to the Nassoni northwest from Natchitoches, that the Chickasaw had killed and enslaved their nation until it was then very small, and that the remnant had been forced to take refuge among the Natchitoch and Nassoni.

The Choctaw enslaved the Choccuma, a small tribe lying between them and the Cherokee, and about 1770 captured and burned their village. The chief and his warriors were slain, and the women and children became the slaves of the conquerors. The Pima of the present southern Arizona took their slaves chiefly from the ranks of the Apache and their allies, and in some degree from the Yuma. These captives were largely children. When not killed they were enslaved. Some of them were kept within the tribe, and were even permitted to marry members of the tribe. But their origin was never forgotten, and the innate superstition of the natives found expression in the declaration of the medicine men that disasters and misfortunes came to the tribe through the presence of these aliens.

In 1540, Mendoza stated that the Pueblo Indians kept their captives for food and for slaves. In the same year, Coronado, on his journey to Cibola, found among the Indians he met an Indian slave who was a native of the country that Soto traversed.

When Du Tisné, in 1719, made his journey west of the Mississippi River, he found the Osage at peace with the Pawnee and at war with the Kansas, Padouca, Aricara and other tribes, who in turn preyed on the Pawnee. The Pawnee were common prey to the tribes on both sides of the Mississippi River. Their nation was not especially small in numbers, but they appear to have been lacking in certain warlike qualities with which some other nations, as the Illinois and Iroquois, were more generously endowed. On this account they were so generally enslaved by their enemies that the term "Pawnee" became synonymous with Indian slave. In 1724, de Bourgmont found the Kansas Indians employing Padouca slaves. De Boucherville, also, on his journey from the Illinois country to Canada, 1728-1729, took with him a little slave for the governor-general of Canada, and was offered other slaves as gifts by the Indians whom he encountered.

In a letter written at Quebec, October 1, 1740, the Marquis de Beauharnois speaks of the Huron bringing slaves from the Flathead and delivering them up to the Outaouac (Ottawa). La Vérendrye, in

1741, was told by the Horse Indians that the Snake Indians had destroyed seventeen of their villages, killed the warriors and women, and carried off the girls and children as slaves.

Of the Wisconsin tribes, the Ottawa and Sauk, at least, were in the habit of making captives of the Pawnee, Osage, Missouri, and even of the distant Mandan, whom they consigned to servitude. The Menominee did not usually engage in these distant wars, but they, and probably other tribes, had Pawnee slaves whom they purchased of the Ottawa, Sauk and others who had captured them. For the sake of convenience, they were called "Pawnees," though some of them were certainly from the Missouri tribes. These captives were usually children.

Beginning with the Tlingit, slavery as an institution, using the term in its strictest sense, existed among all the Northwest coast Indians as far as California. It practically ceased with southern Oregon, although the Hupa of Athapascan stock, and the Nozi (Yanan), both of northern California, practiced it to some extent. Slavery in some form appears to have existed among both the Klamath and the Modoc, and in the Columbia River district as far as the Wallawalla River, where it existed among the Cayuse and the Nez Percés. The Northwest region, embracing the islands and coast occupied by the Tlingit and Haida, and the Chimmesyan, Chinookan, Wakashan, and Salishan tribes, formed the stronghold of the institution. Toward the eastward the institution became modified, as has been shown.

According as an Indian nation proved friendly or unfriendly, the whites used it for their own advantage. Originally the slaves consisted almost entirely of captives taken in war, for there was but little trade among the different nations and tribes until articles of commerce were given by the whites in return for furs and slaves. How the traffic in slaves was affected is seen in the case of the Choctaw and the Chickasaw, the former friends of the French, the latter, of the English. The ill feeling of the two nations was nourished by the international rivalry of their white allies to whom the Indians disposed of many of their captive slaves. The Spaniards of Mexico made slave raids and induced the Indians to do so. La Salle's expedition, found abundant evidence in 1687 of Spanish trade among the Cenis Indians, in their possession of pieces of money, silver spoons, lace, clothes and a bull from Rome exempting the Spaniards in Mexico from fasting during the summer. Some messengers of the Chouman among the Cenis, and the Cenis themselves, told the French of the slave raids and of the cruel treatment of the Indians by the Spaniards to the southward.

Even the Jesuits were not averse to stirring up tribe against tribe. So strong was their interest in the Huron that, for the advancement of the Jesuit cause, it was felt advisable to break up the Iroquois power. Even La Salle advised such a course of action, and urged that the French strengthen the southern Indians by supplying them with firearms and in other ways, so that they might be enabled to defeat the Iroquois, destroy their organization, and carry off their women and children as slaves.

On the other hand, since the Huron were the friends of the French and had been largely converted by the French missionaries, the Jesuits sought to better the lot of the Huron slaves held by the Iroquois, and sent an earnest appeal to the Christians in France to contribute funds for the redemption of the Christian captives. Hennepin's *Narrative* tells of an attempt made by the Jesuits in 1681 to free some Ottawa Indians who were slaves among the Iroquois, by gifts of wampum belts, and by telling the Iroquois that these Ottawa were the children of the governor of the French, and that by holding them they were making war on the French.

The employment to which the Indian slave was put by his Indian owner depended largely upon the section in which the tribe resided. Their use as domestic servants was probably common. Father Fremin tells of a young Iroquois woman who possessed more than twenty personal slaves, whose duty it was to get wood, draw water, cook, and do all other services which their mistress might direct. On the death of the owner who was a Christian, her mother desired that the missionary instruct a sick slave in his religion, so that after death the slave might attend her former mistress in Heaven and perform the same services for her as she had done on earth. Among the Illinois, La Hontan found that two hours after sunset, the slaves covered the fires in the lodge before going to rest. Bartram mentions a southern chief, who had attending him as slaves many Yamasee captives who had been captured by him when young.

Le Jeune found the Huron and Ottawa Indian slaves engaged in minor household duties. In the northwest, enslaved women and children performed the same labor. One other use to which the young women and girls were put, if they did not marry into the tribe, was to serve as the mistresses of their owners.

All the tribes east of the Mississippi River and south of the St. Lawrence River and the Great Lakes practiced agriculture to some extent. They all raised corn, beans, squashes and melons. Consequently the captive slaves worked in the fields with the members of the tribe, caring for the maize and vegetables. The Iroquois used their captives in tilling the fields. Captain John Smith, in speaking of Powhatan's tribe, states that they made war, not for lands and goods, but for women and children, whom they put not to death, but kept as captives, in which captivity they were made to do service. A part of this service consisted in caring for the crops. The Indians of North Carolina kept their slaves at work in the fields. Soto found that the Indians among whom he passed had many foreign slaves whom they employed in tilling the ground. Among the Illinois, La Hontan found the women slaves employed in sowing and reaping.

Slaves were also employed in mining, hunting, fishing, and whatever menial tasks needed to be done about the camp. But few of the tribes worked mines to any extent, yet Joutel, 1687, found the Cenis Indians working slaves in their mines. Hunting and fishing were more important occupations, since they furnished food for the tribe. Among the Iroquois, Huron, Ottawa, and Illinois, such work was partly done by the slaves who often worked with their masters. In the northwest the slave assisted his master in paddling, fishing and hunting. He cut wood, carried water, aided in building houses, etc.

The existence of barter or trade among the different tribes, and among individuals of the same or different tribes, as a means of obtaining slaves has been already noted. Hence it follows that slaves, along with wanpum, furs, etc., served as a medium of exchange in trade. Furthermore, they served as gifts or objects of barter whereby captives belonging to the possessor's tribe might be obtained, and by which an unfriendly tribe or individual might be placated. They were given to the whites to win their favor and friendship. This use of slaves to purchase peace with a stronger tribe was noted by Tonti in the case of the Illinois and Iroquois. The Illinois were too weak to cope with the Iroquois on a certain occasion owing to their young men being away at war, and so by the gift of beaver skins and slaves they were able to arrange a peace. Dubuisson, the French commander in the war of 1712 between the French and allied Indians, and the Ottogami and Mascouten, records a similar use made of their slaves by the Indian allies of the French as a means of appeasing the Potawatami for an old quarrel. From the area about Green Bay in the present State of Wisconsin, De Lignery wrote in 1724 of bringing the warring tribes to an amicable settlement through an interchange of slaves. Other French commanders in the same section used the same means to regain peace. Not only to each other, but to whites as well, were slaves given in order to make reparation for losses in war. In 1684, the Indians offered Du Luth slaves to take the place of some assassinated Frenchmen. In 1724, the Indians at Detroit offered the French commander, by way of truce, two slaves for the same purpose. When slaves were desired for such use, if the tribe possessed none, a raid was often made upon an enemy in order to obtain them. At the time of certain disturbances around Detroit, the Indians in the peace arrangements promised the French that they would make raids on distant nations to obtain slaves whom they would deliver to the French allies to replace their dead.

The treatment of slaves depended upon the individual owner, whose disposition and mood might vary from kindliness to extreme cruelty according to circumstances or caprice, and, still more largely, upon custom. In the northwest slavery had existed for a sufficient length of time before the coming of the whites to modify materially the habits and institutions of the people. It doubtless produced the ideas of rank and caste so generally found among the Indians of that section, but so little known elsewhere among the American Indians. Nevertheless the slaves among the Indians of the northwest were not, as a class, considered any more inferior to their owners than the slaves of the tribes farther east where adoption was more generally practiced. Consequently servitude in that section was of a rather mild type. The same appears to have been true of servitude in general among the Indians. Slaves were probably not generally neglected or abused. Yet there are many testimonials of cruel treatment. Travelers spoke of the slaves of the southern Indians serving and waiting on their masters with signs of the most abject fear, as tame, mild and tractable, without will or power to act but as directed by their masters. The slave was expected to obey his master blindly and without disputing. In this connection it must be understood that enslavement of captives in war was in itself a kindly act on the part of the captors, determined partly by the need of laborers and additional members in the tribe, partly by the use which the victors could make of these captives in traffic with other tribes and with the whites, and partly by mere whim. Otherwise, the prisoners were tortured and killed as an expression of hatred, or as a means of obtaining revenge for injury. To instil fear into them, slaves were often compelled to observe the torture of their fellow captives who were condemned to death. La Salle relates an instance in which slaves were forced to eat one of their own nation, a victim of such torture. Among the Cenis such a custom was followed, and it is quite possible that this method of producing subjection was consistent with the habitual cruelty of most tribes.

Precautions were taken to prevent the escape of slaves. The southern Indians were accustomed to mutilate the feet of their slaves either by cutting away a part of the foot, or by cutting the nerves and sinews just above the ankle or instep. The slave was thus prevented from running rapidly, and if he should escape, the tracks of his mutilated feet were easily recognizable.

The life or death of Indian slaves depended upon either the council or the women. The captives were apportioned by the council to different individuals of the tribe, usually at the request of the women, who often preferred to adopt captives into their families to replace lost husbands and sons, rather than to revenge themselves for the loss of relatives by demanding the torture and death of the slaves. After such distribution, the life or death of a slave depended entirely upon the will of the owner. Among a barbarous people, a slave's life naturally had but little value. Sick and useless slaves were often put to death, and trivial faults might be punished in the same way. The Jesuit missionaries said of the Iroquois: "When a barbarian has split the head of his slave with a hatchet," he says, "It is a dead dog—there is nothing to be done but to cast it upon the dung hill."

On the other hand, the Jesuits record certain instances of kindness shown to slaves by the Iroquois and other tribes. One important difference existed between the Indian slavery as practiced by the Indians themselves, and that in existence among the whites. Among the Indians the question of social equality did not determine the relation of the slave to the master. The Indian slaves were always considered eligible for adoption into the tribes as actual members, in order to replete the numbers reduced by war, famine, disease or other cause. Among the Iroquois certain chosen slaves married into the tribe and became heads of families after the death of their owners. They led a tolerably easy life, but were still considered as slaves, and had no voice, either active or passive, in the public councils. Still others, who had been the richest and most important in their own villages, received no reward from their masters except food and clothing. A certain amount of liberty seems to have been accorded these slaves, for the Jesuits were allowed to work among them sometimes as openly as among the members of the tribe. Bartram found that among the southern Indians the slaves were dressed better than their owners, and were allowed to marry among themselves; but they remained slaves for life.

There were several ways by which Indian slaves could obtain their freedom. Among the Huron a young brave could marry his mother's slave, and his parents had no right to hinder him. By becoming his wife the slave became a free woman. Among the southern Indians the children of slave parents were free and were considered in every respect equal to their parents' masters. Among the western Indians, upon the death of a savage, his slaves intermarried with others of their kind and lived in a separate hut as a sign that they were free since they had no master to serve. The children of such marriages were adopted into the tribe and became the children of the nation, since they were born in the country and village of the tribe. The Indians believed that the children should not be held as slaves since they contributed nothing to their creation. In the northwest, the distinction between slave and free man was generally sharply drawn with regard to marriage, for the slave usually could not marry the free man or woman, though the Makah men frequently married slave women. The children of such marriages appear to have held an equivocal position between free men and slaves.

The most common mode of acquiring freedom was through adoption into the tribes. Among the tribes of the Great Plains and the Atlantic Slope, adoption seems to have been universally practiced. The slaves adopted usually consisted of war captives, who in some instances were adopted wholesale, or who, after a period of servitude in the tribe, had proved themselves possessed of certain desirable qualities, such as bravery and strength in war or the chase. The adopted person became in every respect the peer of his fellow-tribesmen. If he showed his ability he might become of high rank in the tribe. If he were a poor hunter, a poor provider, or, above all, if he turned out to be a coward, he was despised and treated according to his demerits, probably worse than if he had been born a member of the tribe. Still, he was a member of the tribe and remained a free man, though he was deposed from man's estate and made a woman. Adopted persons who showed little ability, were sometimes made to serve in the families of the influential and prominent men of the tribe; but such persons were free, even though they performed menial labor.

In some sections, a captive could not become a member of a tribe without a relationship of some sort; and to obtain this, he had to be adopted by a woman as her child. The captive took the kinship name under the fiction that he was younger to every living person of the tribe at the time, and that all persons subsequently born were "younger" to him. If the captive belonged to a tribe of hereditary enemies who had from time immemorial been designated by opprobrious terms, such as cannibals, liars, snakes, etc., it might be that the captive was doomed to perpetual " younger brotherhood," and could never exercise authority over any person within the tribe, though such person might have been born after the adoption of the captive. Usually, though not invariably, the captives adopted were children. They might ultimately become useful members of the tribe, and by their virtues even win rank in kinship. A captive might thus pass from slavery to freedom.

Occasionally the settlement of intertribal difficulties resulted in the freeing of the captives by the victors, with permission to return to their former homes. Such freedom might be given to a whole tribe that had been conquered, or to single individuals. In either case the stigma of disgrace attached to the condition of slavery still remained, and leaders of the tribe were preferably chosen from those who had never been slaves. Exchange or ransom was common. If a tribe declared war against another formally, which happened but rarely, slaves were sent with the notification of such fact to the enemy, and were given their freedom if they promised not to take up arms against their former masters. Freedom was given for performing certain services against their masters' enemies, such as influencing their own tribe against such enemies.

In concluding this account of the institution of slavery among the Indians of the present United States it should be stated that no attempt has been made to treat the subject in detail. The purpose of the chapter is to show the existence of slavery and something of its nature, so as to obtain an historical setting for the discussion of the enslavement of the Indians by the whites which is to follow. Relatively few of the Indian tribes have been mentioned, but these covered sufficient territory to show that the custom of slave-holding was practically universal. The familiarity of the Europeans who came to America with the institution of slavery, and the finding of the same custom among the Indians themselves, make their carrying on of the practice quite natural.

CHAPTER II. ENSLAVEMENT BY THE SPANIARDS

IN their attitude toward the Indians the Spaniards simply applied the theory of their time regarding slavery. The taking of slaves was then considered part of any expedition of discovery or conquest. The high authority of the Church sanctioned the institution of slavery to the extent that the leading theologians had declared all barbarous and infidel nations who shut their ears to the truths of Christianity, fair objects of rapine, captivity and slavery.

The general feeling regarding the relation of the Indians to the Spaniards is well expressed by Hernando de Escalante Fontanedo, who was with Menendez in Florida as interpreter. In writing of Florida, he declared it his belief that the Indians "can never be made submissive and become Christians"; so he advocated that they all be taken, "placed on ships, and scattered throughout the various islands, and even on the Spanish Main, where they might be sold as His Majesty sells his vessels to the grandees in Spain."

Given this attitude on the subject it was but natural that the enslavement of the American Indians should begin with the discovery of the Antilles, and that it should be continued by the explorers on the mainland. The Spanish exploring expeditions were war expeditions in the sense that they aimed to conquer and retain for the crown the territory through which they passed. All these expeditions captured and retained Indians as slaves. Yet in some cases it might be difficult to determine whether the Indians enslaved were captives taken in actual warfare, or whether they were merely kidnapped by the expedition passing through their territory. Often the expeditions possessed the double character of a war party and a kidnapping company.

The enslavement of the Indians by the Spaniards in the early years of occupation was legalized by a royal decree which declared the act to be in accord with the laws of God and man, and justified it on the ground that Indians could otherwise not be reclaimed from idolatry and converted to Christianity. Consistent with its assertion the home government made careful provision, in the various patents issued to the explorers, for the spiritual welfare of the enslaved Indians.

These patents commonly made provision for the acquisition of Indian slaves. That of Ponce de Leon, February 23, 1512, authorizing his voyage of discovery and colonization, provided that the Indians on the islands he might discover should be distributed among the members of the expedition, that the discoverers should be well provided for in the first allotment of slaves, and that they should "derive whatever advantage might be secured thereby." The "cédula," issued to Lucas Vasquez de Ayllon, in 1523, authorized him to purchase prisoners of war held as slaves by the natives, to employ them on his farms and export them as he saw fit, without the payment of any duty whatever upon them; formal apportionment of the natives was expressly forbidden. In the patent to Soto, also, it was required that he should carry with him "the religious and priests, who shall be appointed by us, for the instruction of the natives of that province in our holy Catholic faith."

The idea of Christianizing the natives was applied to both free and slave Indians. The taking of captives by force, and then Christianizing them was the continuation of what was known as "the exercise of a just and pious doctrine against pagans and heathens" a doctrine common to other nations as well as to Spain. The patent of Ponce de Leon, however, made no provision for Christianizing the Indians. His instructions from the crown required him to summon the natives by "requisition" to embrace the Catholic faith and yield to the king of Spain under threat of sword and slavery. Consequently the Spanish explorers within the present limits of the United States continued the policy of enslaving Indians pursued by their countrymen elsewhere in the New World.

A Spanish ship sailing under Esteban Gomez, a Portuguese, in 1525, coasted along the shores of North America between Nova Scotia and Florida, seeking the northwest passage, and carried a few Indians back to Spain. In April, 1528, the expedition of Pánfilo de Narvaez landed near the entrance to Tampa Bay on the west coast of Florida. From this point a portion of the expedition started into the interior. The first Indians met seemed unfriendly, and five or six of them were seized. On one occasion, a cacique, or chief, was held prisoner. But supplies failed and discouragement followed, so the number of Indians taken was not great. In 1538, also, an expedition sent out by Hernando de Soto brought two natives from Florida to Cuba, where they were held to learn the Spanish language in order that they might act as guides and interpreters for the expedition of the following year.

In 1539, Soto himself landed in the Bay of Espiritu Santo in Florida for the purpose of conquest. He had served under Pizarro in Peru, and his methods were those learned from his master. To insure success all opposition must be overcome, so, with the expedition were taken blood-hounds, chains and iron collars for the catching and holding of Indian slaves. The expedition was military in nature, hence it was natural that force and conquest should precede conciliation. There is no doubt that one of the purposes of Soto was to capture Indian slaves. He had chosen as his lieutenant, a rich resident of the town of Trinidad in Cuba, Vasco Porcallo de Figueroa, who had come to Florida with the object of obtaining Indian slaves for his estates. But slaves were not easily obtainable near the coast, so Porcallo returned home shortly after. Soto himself was a slave owner. Among his possessions in Cuba were Indian slaves, whom he employed as herdsmen and in getting gold. In some cases, the Indian chiefs through whose territories Soto and his men were passing, furnished slaves. At other times, they, both men and women, were taken by force. Narrators relate the capture and distribution of such women in groups of one hundred to three hundred. Among the captives were a queen and a cacique.

After the survivors of Soto's expedition had reached Mexico, Viceroy Mendoza dispatched the Franciscan, Fray Marcos de Niza, in 1539, to inform the native tribes that an effectual stop had been put to the enslavement of the Indians. Some of the friar's party reached Hawaikuh, the southernmost of the seven cities of Cibola. The account which the friar gave on his return, induced the viceroy to send out another expedition in the following year, 1540. The command of this was given to Francisco Vasquez de Coronado.

But Coronado did not carry out the intention of Mendoza regarding the Indians. The records of his expedition do not indicate the number of his slaves as equal to that in Soto's expedition, yet Coronado was a man of his time, and Mendoza was ultra humanitarian. When Tiguex was conquered and plundered, March,

1541, Coronado imprisoned and made servants of all the people, one hundred and fifty men, women and children who were in it.

Still other Spanish expeditions were nothing more than slave raids or kidnapping excursions. In 1520, Lucas Vasquez de Ayllon, a wealthy resident of Hispaniola, determined to send out a ship for the purpose of exploring the section north of that covered by Ponce de Leon in 1513. His caravel met among the Bahamas a second ship sent out by another resident of Hispaniola to obtain Indian slaves, The two vessels joined company, and proceeded toward the continent, which they reached June 25, 1521, in the neighborhood of the River Jordan (the present Santee or Combahee) and the cape afterward called Cabo de Santa Elena. By gifts and proffers of friendship, the Indians were lured on board, and the ships, having obtained a full cargo, set sail for Hispaniola.

After the collapse of Narvaez's expedition, Cabeza de Vaca wandered through the southwest, hoping to reach Spanish settlements. As he proceeded, he met, thirty leagues from St. Miguel, a Spanish expedition coming from the south, from which the Indians were fleeing lest they be captured and held as slaves. Though this slave hunting expedition met with considerable success, its leaders, nevertheless, wished to enslave the friendly Indians who had guided Cabeza de Vaca and his companions thither. Cabeza de Vaca relates that he continued his journey to Compostella in the company, among others, of six Christians and five hundred Indian slaves.

Such expeditions from Mexico were continued until well into the colonial period. The Indians whom La Salle met, 1684–1688, told him they knew whites toward the west, a cruel, wicked nation, who depopulated the country round them.

It will be seen that the custom of enslaving Indians was general among the Spanish discoverers and explorers. Not to have followed such a custom would have been acting contrary to the spirit of the times. Church and State sanctioned it. The need for a servile class, and the supply of natives near at hand to meet the demand, made enslavement only a matter of course. Slavery existed among the native tribes themselves and the tribal chiefs readily furthered the policy of the Spaniards by furnishing them with additional slaves and prisoners. Consequently, when the action of the Spaniards is viewed from the moral standpoint of the time, no condemnation can be attached to their practice of enslaving the aborigines.

Some of the Indians used by the Spanish explorers were obtained from the Indian tribes through purchase or trade. Such a method of obtaining them was advisable when the tribes were friendly and it was not politic to arouse their enmity. Prisoners and slaves, accordingly, both men and women, were traded or presented as gifts, along with other merchandise, to the Spaniards.

In all the exploring expeditions, the need of guides, interpreters, camp laborers and burden bearers was imperative. At one time, Soto possessed eight hundred Indians, given him by an Indian chief, to act as porters. The leaders must have some means of rewarding the services of their soldiers. Gold and other desirable objects were scarce. Indian slaves helped satisfy this need. Soto had the foresight, before setting out on his journey of exploration, to provide guides, consisting of Indian slaves seized in the territory which he expected to traverse, and seized others to act in this capacity as occasion required. Slaves were used for the same purpose by Coronado. The women slaves were used largely as cooks and as mistresses. Soto apportioned women slaves among his men. The narrators relate the capture and distribution of such women in groups of one hundred to three hundred. Women were sometimes given by the chiefs to the white men for this purpose, as in the case of Coronado's expedition.

In general, the treatment of slaves must have depended upon the individual owners. It must be noted that it was held an act of clemency on the part of the victor to enslave rather than to slaughter the captives taken in war, for, according to the ideas of the time, conquered enemies were at the disposal of the conquerors. In the case of Soto's expedition, the treatment of the slaves appears, on the whole to have been kind. After the death of Soto, the Spaniards decided to quit the scene of exploration. The Indian slaves could not be taken, for there was no way of transporting them, so it was decided to dismiss them, except about three hundred belonging to the leader Moscoso and some of his friends. To satisfy others who desired to take their Indians with them, Moscoso granted permission to take the slaves as far as the mouth of the river. The owners, moved by an humanitarian motive, and preferring to give up the Indians before sailing, rather than to free them at the mouth of the river to become the prey of enemies, set free five hundred men, women and children. Many of them had learned to speak Spanish, had become Christians, and were so attached to their Spanish owners that they wept bitterly at the separation. This scene indicates an affection between master and slaves that would exist only with kind treatment. It has been held that Soto's treatment of the Indians was probably better than that practiced by most of the discoverers—a treatment at least partly dictated by policy, for the Indians of the section traversed by him were superior to those of Central and South America, both in courage and perseverance. Those Indians who continued the journey with the Spaniards were set free by the viceroy on reaching Mexico. In the siege of Tigeux Coronado's men cared for those Indians who, in trying to escape, were overcome by wounds and cold. Special cases of cruelty occurred. Strict vigilance and severe punishment were necessary to prevent treachery on the part of the slaves. The cruelty of the age was expressed by throwing a lying and treacherous Indian to the dogs, by cutting off the hands and noses of some, and by keeping others in chains. On the whole, however, the treatment of the slaves was probably no more cruel than that shown slaves elsewhere, nor than would be expected considering the tendency of the age, the nature of the owners, largely soldiers and adventurers, and the incapacity and disinclination of the natives for many kinds of labor.

The manumission of slaves depended partly on the individual owners, partly on the leaders of the various expeditions. An instance of the latter kind we have already seen in the case of Moscoso freeing the slaves when quitting the scene of Soto's expedition. But such an incident was the exception rather than the rule, for slaves were the personal property of their individual owners, and subject to their action.

By the law of 1543, the Spanish government intended to end Indian slavery in its American dominions, but the law was ineffectual. The American possessions were too far removed for thorough control by the home government. When Spain took final possession of Louisiana, in 1769, O'Reilly discovered that the French held many Indian slaves, and in a proclamation, which he issued in 1770, declared this to be "contrary to the wise and pious laws of Spain."

While not at once declaring these Indian slaves to be free, he ordered that the actual proprietors should not dispose, in any manner whatever, of those whom they held, unless it were to give them their freedom, until the orders of his Majesty on the subject should be received, and further, that all owners of Indian slaves should make a declaration of name and nation of the Indians so held in slavery by them, and the price at which they valued such slaves. This proclamation was generally understood by the French settlers of upper Louisiana as emancipating all the Indian slaves; yet the latter remained in slavery, either voluntarily or otherwise. They obtained some benefit from O'Reilly's decree, however, for when they escaped they were not returned to slavery, and when they sued for their freedom they received it. Thus, in 1786, Governor Miró, in a case that came before him from St. Louis, rendered a judgment that liberated several such slaves. This judgment reminded Lieutenant Governor Cruzat that the ordinance of O'Reilly was not being obeyed, so in June, 1787, he issued a proclamation that Indians could not be held in slavery under the ordinance of 1770, and declared that he "judged it expedient to repeat the aforesaid ordinance, so that the public might know its tenor in order to conform to it." Accordingly the said ordinance was ordered to be read, published and posted in the customary places. No order on this subject was received from the king, so Baron Carondelet, 1794, ordered two Indian slaves to abide with their masters until the royal will was expressed. In the same year, however, he ordered another Indian slave to be released.

It is evident, therefore, that it was not through direct executive decree that Indian slavery passed out of existence in Spanish territory within the present limits of the United States. In fact, from the instance cited in connection with Louisiana, it is seen that it did not pass out of existence until after the colonial period. Certain causes, however, contributed to its decline. Great number of Indians could be hired, at very small wages, to perform labor of any extent. Still another cause, which was less effective perhaps in Spanish territory than in that of France and England, was the use of negro slaves. The labor of the blacks was early found to be more profitable than that of the Indians, and as early as the founding of St. Augustine, Menendez imported into Florida five hundred negro slaves. Otherwise, the labor of building that town would have fallen on the white men, and on the Indians whom he could impress.

From the earliest days of Spanish occupancy, the spiritual welfare of the Indians was of much concern to the Spanish Church and State. The materialization of such an interest was largely accomplished by the establishment of missions throughout the Spanish territory from Florida to California, chiefly through the labors of the Franciscans. The endeavors of the missionaries resulted in the establishment by 1615 of twenty missions in Florida and the dependent coast region. By 1655, the Christian Indian population of northern Florida and the Georgia coast was estimated at 26,000. By 1630, there were more than 60,000 "converts" in the Pueblo missions of New Mexico and Arizona. In California, the missions, the first of which was founded at San Diego in 1769, continued in a fairly prosperous condition until 1834.

These large numbers of barbarian neophytes were presided over in each of the missions by a very small number of monks who directed the religious and industrial activities of their Indian charges. It was necessary that a mission should be self-supporting. The Indians gathered at these centers voluntarily, and submitted to the routine life of the missions. But the natives were ignorant and incapable, and the monks were in consequence the directing and guiding force among a population which responded in a mechanical sort of way. The natural result was that the mission life developed into a kind of slavery. The life of a California mission, though of later date, and more fully developed than the earlier missions of colonial times, affords a picture of the general condition of affairs.

The Indians constructed the buildings, planted and cultivated the fruit trees and vineyards, tended the cattle, made pottery, wove cloths and performed, in fact, all the manual labor that was necessarily required in an extensive colony. In return, they received food, clothing and lodging, were instructed in the Church doctrines and observances, and were taught dancing and music and occasionally the rudiments of reading, writing and arithmetic. Their life was a regular routine, and though material comfort was generally in evidence, still the Indian neophytes were never allowed to act on their own initiative.

Beyond their existence from day to day, they received no pecuniary reward for their labors, any more than if they had been slaves.

The Indians of the missions were generally tractable, but occasionally the desire for their former life of freedom brought reaction and rebellions; or, incited and aided by the wild tribes, they rose and destroyed the missions. The revolt of the Pima in 1750 is a case in point.

The "alcaldes," or local officials to whom the king had entrusted the protection of the Indians, instead of protecting them, preyed upon them for their own profit. These men, like many of the colonists themselves, were often of an inferior class, and too far from the central government to feel any special fear at disobeying the laws that the home government might make with regard to the natives. Accordingly the Indians were often induced to run into debt, and had in consequence to mortgage or sell whatever property they possessed. They thus became subject to whatever impositions the officials chose to put upon them. In 1792, Fray Juan Agustin de Morfi complained to the viceroy of New Spain that from each pueblo in their respective jurisdictions, the "alcaldes" in Texas were accustomed to levy weekly contributions of produce; that they required the Indians to perform free labor upon their estates; that they demanded heavy tolls from each pueblo at harvest time; that the Indian women were forced to grind the alcaldes' grain; that some officials required tithes of fleeces and compelled the Indians to weave them; and that the Indians had to serve as mule drivers and care for the animals of the "alcaldes." The attitude of the "alcaldes" toward the Indians, furthermore, was repeated by the officials of the "presidios," or frontier posts.

The same method of obtaining cheap labor was followed by the colonists. Frequent raids were made upon the "rancherías," or Indian settlements, to secure agricultural workers, herdsmen and domestic servants. Children were usually in demand, but adults also were taken. The practice continued, indeed, until late in the eighteenth century.

INDIAN SLAVERY

CHAPTER III. ENSLAVEMENT BY THE FRENCH

IN the French colonies of America, Indian slavery was never authorized by legal declaration during the early colonial period. In fact, the matter received no attention whatever from the home government. Such lack of notice on the part of the monarch was due to the insignificance of American affairs in general, and to the unimportance of the institution of Indian slavery in particular. Gradually, however, as the matter began to assume importance in the system of trade, through the influence of the trading companies certain indirect royal action was taken in the eighteenth century, and this action recognized the existing institution as legal. The modifications which the king sought to accomplish in it did not aim to destroy the institution, but rather tended to make it better suited to the requirements of trade.

Some doubt appears to have existed regarding the legal status of Indian slaves, and, in order to remove it, Jacques Raudot, the intendant at Quebec, decreed in April, 1709, that "all the Pawnis and Negroes, who have been bought and who shall be purchased hereafter, shall belong in full proprietorship to those who have purchased them as their slaves." The state of unrest caused by the "coureurs de bois" and others stirring up the tribes in order to take captives for sale to the French as slaves, interfered with the success of the trading corporation then in possession of Louisiana, and on October 25, 1720, the Company of the Indies issued a command from Paris, stating that such action was contrary to the command of the king, and harmful to both the commercial welfare of the Company and the establishments which it hoped to make in the territory of the Illinois, Missouri and Arkansas tribes. The Sieur de Bourgmont, in the service of the Company in that area, was directed to arrest and confiscate the merchandise of the "voyageurs" who should come to trade within the confines of his jurisdiction without first obtaining permission and declaring to him the motives with which they wished to trade. Bienville, then in immediate charge of the colony in Louisiana, was directed to execute this order of the Company at once, and all other officers as well were enjoined to carry it out and to give any aid and assistance to M. de Bourgmont which he might require in fulfilling his instructions.

On July 23, 1745, the royal council at Paris sanctioned the possession of Indian slaves by declaring that all slaves who might follow the enemy to the colonies of France, and their effects, should belong to his most Christian Majesty. After the acquisition of Canada the Parliament of Great Britain showed itself favorable to the importation of slaves into the colonies. Accordingly, the forty-seventh article of the capitulation of September 8, 1760, provided: "The negroes and Pawnees, of both sexes, shall remain in their quality of slaves, in the possession of French and Canadians to whom they belong; they shall be at liberty to keep them in their service in the colony, or to sell them; and they shall also continue to bring them up in the Roman religion."

Public opinion in France never concerned itself with the matter of Indian slavery. There appears to have been no opposition to it, either in France or in the French colonies of America. Public opinion early countenanced the institution of slavery in the colonies without distinction of color or race. It was negro slavery that brought profit to the trader as well as to the colonist. The Indian slave in the French colonies possessed no champion, such as the Indian slave in the Spanish territory had in Las Casas. Within the French territory under discussion, negro slavery continued, without meeting violent opposition, as long as the territory remained under French control. And with it continued Indian slavery, gradually growing weaker as negro slavery grew stronger, and so less likely to attract attention.

Much of the French exploration was carried on by the missionaries. Slave holding was not inconsistent with the belief of these religious travelers. Two objects inspired their zeal: the "greater glory of God," and "the influence and credit of the order of Jesus," of which many of them were members. To the missionaries about to start from Paris to explore the Ottawa country, the direction was given: "Remember it is Christ and the Cross you are seeking, and if you aim at anything else, you will get nothing but affliction for body and mind." The Jesuit held that if the object was good, the action was right. It would redound to the glory of God to convert any heathen, bond or free; therefore, slave holding by a monk was legitimate.

The records do not show any great numbers of slaves owned by the missionary explorers. There are certain reasons why this was so.

Abnegation of self was a part of the Jesuitic doctrine, so the monk could have no need for any considerable number of personal attendants. He possessed no mines or lands for the working of which slaves could be used. What services the fathers could not perform in the extension of their faith, were performed partly by servants brought from France, and partly by "donnés," or those who voluntarily gave their labor. At the missions and in the Indian villages where the missionaries stayed, the Indians rendered them free service and furnished them with supplies. Then, too, the Indian domestic did not prove very satisfactory. The slave was a subject for conversion, but the French missionary did not spend much time on the conversion of single individuals. He aimed rather to collect the heathen in groups about a religious center, and to guide and teach them somewhat after the manner of his brethren in Paraguay. Yet we find that the French missionaries possessed some Indian slaves. It would not do to refuse to save any soul, neither was it advisable to risk the chance of offending any Indian, whatever his rank, who might make them the gift of a slave. Most of the slaves held by the missionaries appear to have been gifts. Sometimes to accept such a slave was to save the person from death. Some of the slaves were purchased. By teaching them the French language, and the principles of the Christian Church, the clergy hoped to make missionaries of some of them, and so extend the scope of their religion.

The chief, though not the earliest, source of Indian slaves among the French was that of captives taken in war with the Indian tribes. For many years after the coming of the French to Louisiana, they and the Natchez Indians lived in friendly intercourse. Minor Indian troubles in 1711 and 1715 resulted in the enslavement and transportation of certain Indians to Cape François on the island of Haiti. The hostilities begun with the Natchez Indians in 1715 continued intermittently until 1740. In 1730, because of ill treatment by M. du Chapart, governor of Fort Rosalie, who wished the site of a Natchez village on which to build a town, and because of other abuses, the Natchez rose against the French and massacred over two hundred of them. Governor Périer formed an army and advanced against them in their fort. The Natchez offered to leave the place if their lives were spared. Their offer was accepted, but they were detained as prisoners, all but twenty who escaped. About four hundred and fifty of the tribe, including the Great Sun, the Little Sun and several of the principal war chiefs, were captured and carried to New Orleans. The women and children were retained as slaves on the plantations. Some of the prisoners were burned in New Orleans. The Great Sun, the Little Sun, their families, and more than four hundred of the captives, were sent at once to Cape François, Haiti, and most of them sold to the planters as slaves. The two chiefs and their families were retained as prisoners on the island. On April 22, 1731, the minister informed the Company that, in his opinion, the only solution of the matter lay in selling as slaves the survivors of the two families. The registers of the Company contain the following record: "It was resolved to order the sale of the survivors of the said two families of Natchez Indians."

The Natchez war was the most important of those between French and Indians in Louisiana. There were, however, minor difficulties, from time to time, in which the same policy of enslaving the captive Indians was followed by the French. The war with the Fox Indians, 1712, serves as an example of these lesser troubles. By 1720, war had broken out between the French and the Chickasaw, whom the English had stirred up. An intermittent warfare with this tribe and others continued in 1724, 1728, 1736 (with a peace in 1740), 1750, and 1752. Captives were enslaved by both sides. Some of these were left with the Indians to dispose of at will. Others were kept among the French as slaves.

During the period of colonial history, each European nation was in alliance, from time to time, with various Indian tribes. In time of war with other tribes, the allied Indians took an active part, and not infrequently they were urged on to hostilities by their white friends for various reasons. One of these reasons was to obtain war captives to give to the whites for slaves. In 1698, Tonti had encouraged the Illinois, who were in alliance with the French, to capture and enslave the Iroquois Indians and so break their power. La Salle favored the same course. In 1708, the Canadian French were exciting the Indians about Kaskaskia to wage war with each other, and were on the spot to get slaves to sell to the English. The Marquis de Vaudreuil, governor-general of Canada, in 1706 demanded of the Ottawa of Detroit certain captives as slaves for the allied Sonnontouan to replace their men slain by the Ottawa, and others to be slaves to the French, in return for a missionary and a French deserter they had killed. The slaves were duly presented in 1707. The demands of the governor-general were part of a military plan to form an alliance of the western tribes with the French, and continued the Indian custom of giving slaves to make reparation for injuries committed or for foes slain. Thus the allied Indians were satisfied, and a token of subjection was obtained from the Ottawa. As late as 1723, de Vaudreuil was accused of urging on the Abnaki against the Illinois to get slaves for him. Apparently, such action was as agreeable to the Indians as to the French. An Indian orator of the Arkansas tribe, in his address given in honor of Bossu's arrival in 1762, said: "We warriors will strike the common enemy to get prisoners which shall serve as slaves."

Sometimes the French went still further, and demanded that conquered tribes make war on other tribes in order to get captives for them to take the place of Frenchmen killed during the war. Such a condition Sieur de Louvigny placed on the conquered Fox Indians in 1716.

As already observed, kidnapping was the means earliest adopted by all the European nations for taking Indians as slaves. In 1524, accordingly, Verrazano attempted to capture an Indian family consisting of an old woman, a young girl and six children, on the northeast coast of North America. But the girl proved so intractable that the soldiers were forced to give up the attempt to take the whole family to the ship, and finally carried away but one small boy who was too young to make any resistance. The purpose of Verrazano's expedition was to obtain for France a place in the discoveries in which the rival powers, Spain, Portugal and England were engaged. Some proof that the expedition reached the New World was desirable. A native would furnish it.

In Cartier's first expedition, 1534, he seized some of the natives and carried them on board his ships. The relations with the Indians were so friendly that he was able, by gifts and explanations, to persuade them that he meant no harm. Two of them were finally detained on board and carried to France. On the second expedition, in 1535, Cartier, replying to the request of the chief, Taiguragui, that the

French carry away another chief, Agona, declared that the king of France had forbidden him to bring back either man or woman, and permitted him to bring to France only two or three little boys to learn the language. But these pretended instructions did not prevent Cartier from seizing Taiguragui and other chiefs for the purpose of carrying them to France. On the outcry of the Indians against such an act, he promised that the chiefs should be well treated, and that after visiting France for the purpose of telling the king about the land of Saguenay, they should be returned to their own country within the space of twelve months.

On his setting out for the New World in 1562, the queen of France commanded Ribaut to bring back some of the natives. In obedience to her command, Ribaut attempted to detain two of the natives on board ship to carry them to France, but the savages managed to escape and swam to shore.

Some of the Indians kidnapped by the explorers mentioned were slaves only in a modified sense. They were not put to servile labor, yet they were deprived of their liberty and were at the disposal of their captors. Some were held as objects of curiosity. Others were taken for a definite purpose: to furnish information regarding their native country, and to serve as interpreters in later expeditions. For such a reason La Harpe, in 1719, in his journey in the southwest, when returning to the coast, resolved to capture some of the Indians, hoping that by good treatment he might induce them to allow him to settle in their country and to carry out his plans. Under the pretence of landing to obtain water for his ships, he seized a dozen or more, and sailed for Mobile.

The Indians soon became suspicious of the explorers and traders, especially in the sections where more than one of the rival races carried on exploration and trade. Such a state of affairs Du Tisné found in 1719, when he was badly received by the Pawnee whom the Osage had told that his purpose was to entrap Indians for slaves.

The great purpose of the French in the new world was trade. Their expeditions, excluding those of the missionaries, were commercial in nature. With them gold hunting was not a primary consideration, as was the case with the Spaniards, and that for the simple reason that no gold could be found. Nor were they seeking a refuge from persecution like the English. The great fur trade was being developed by them. This trade was carried on with the Indians, and in all sections where captives in war or kidnapped Indians were purchased from the natives, such purchase was usually a part of the trade in furs.

The custom of purchasing Indians originated with the early explorers and discoverers. Sometimes such a purchase was made for a purely commercial reason: to obtain a slave to perform some certain labor. At other times the buyer was moved by an humanitarian motive: to save an Indian from torture or death at the hands of his captors. The purchased Indian might then be allowed to return to his own tribe and be retained as a slave at the will of his new master. In 1678, Du Lhut, when setting out from Montreal on his travels westward, bought an Indian to act as a guide. Du Tisné, in 1719, similarly acquired some slaves from a chief at Natchitoches. In 1724, de Bourgmont purchased a considerable number of slaves from the Kansas tribe. Mention is made of fifteen at one time, six at another. For these he was forced to pay double price, as the Indians stated that the year before, a Frenchman had given such a price to a party of Illinois who were with them. Sometimes the slaves obtained by these explorers and traders were used in their own expeditions. At other times, they were sent back to the settlement along with other merchandise. De Bourgmont sent some of those whom he purchased back to New Orleans. La Vérendrye, also, in 1731, sent back slaves to the French settlements, and in writing of his action implied that he thought he deserved much credit for furnishing the colonists with slaves.

Until well into the latter half of the eighteenth century Indian slaves were held by the settlers of Detroit, who obtained them in trade with friendly Indians who in turn took them in war with the Pawnee, Osage, Choctaw and other western tribes. In 1741, the so-called "Nation of the Serpent" entirely destroyed seventeen villages, killed all the men and older women, made slaves of the young women, and traded them for horses and other merchandise. A report to the home government in 1720, concerning Natchitoches, declared that the most extensive commerce which could be carried on with the Indians of that section, would be in slaves, horses, skins, etc. Another report sent by La Salle told of the Alabama Indians bringing twenty-seven or twenty-eight Mobile Indian women and children into the colony, and disposing of them to the French.

The friendly and allied Indians appreciated the results to be obtained from the sale of their captives to the whites, and not only sold them to the "coureurs de bois" and other traveling traders, but took them directly to the French settlement for sale, as is shown in the preceding paragraph. Apparently all the leading French settlements afforded a ready market for such slaves. Mobile furnishes a case in point. In November, 1706, a party of Ouacha arrived in the settlement bringing some Abnaki captives for sale. In the same month, also, some Choctaw brought to the settlement Cahouita and Altamaha captives for the same purpose.

It was the Jesuit and French missionaries who first advocated the purchase of Indian captives by the traders, in order to prevent their being put to death. By putting them in a mild condition of servitude they hoped to place them in a position where they would be Christianized. Both Tonti and La Salle advised such a course of action.

The colonists favored the same action for a more commercial reason. The French of Kaskaskia, in 1708, were urging the allied Indians to war, and were on the spot to obtain captives to sell as slaves to the English. De Vaudreuil, governor-general of Canada, throughout the first quarter of the eighteenth century was urging the Abnaki to wage war on the Illinois to obtain slaves for him.

An important factor in the French colonial trade was the "coureurs de bois." These men, having cut loose from civilization, wandered at will among the Indians, trading for the various commodities which they could dispose of in the settlements of either the French or English colonies. One of these commodities was Indian slaves, obtained for the most part from the tribes who had captured them in war. Judging from the number of these white men of the woods, their unrestrained life, and the evidence given by the men of the time, it seems not unlikely that this feature of colonial trade produced a considerable portion of the Indian slaves used by the French. If the "coureurs de bois" did not find a sufficient number of slaves among the tribes they visited, they not infrequently stirred up the tribes to war, so that they might obtain the captives for sale. On

July 25, 1707, La Salle wrote from Fort Louis to the Minister of Marine that the "coureurs de bois" from Canada were thus stirring up the Indian tribes against each other, in order to obtain Indian slaves to sell in Louisiana. The work of the "coureurs de bois" was, however, by no means limited to Louisiana, but extended over all the area claimed by the French. The desire of the English for Indian slaves afforded an opportunity for profit that could not be rejected. They always found a ready market for their Indian slaves with the English of the Carolina country. The control of the French officials over this wandering class was always slight, and since there was practically no export trade in Indians to be had in Louisiana, and since all the Indians whom they obtained could not be disposed of in the colony, they turned to the English colonies for the purpose.

Some effort was made by the French officials to prevent this trade, but the attempt met with indifferent success. It was not the traffic in human beings which disturbed them, but the fact that their enemy, the English, were profiting by the transaction. In 1714, a report of Cadillac to the home government lamented both his inability to restrain the French allied Indians from trading with the English in slaves and other commodities, and also his embarrassment at not being able to prevent the French colonists from trading with the English in skins and Indian slaves. Such opposition, however, was not general among the French colonial officials. Some of the most prominent ones were engaged in this same slave trade with the English, even when appearing to be opposed to it. In 1708, Bienville ordered the Canadian French to cease exciting the Indians of Kaskaskia to wage war on each other to obtain slaves for them. Yet, in the same year, he proposed, since the French would not cultivate the land, to obtain the needful supply of labor by seizing Indians and sending them to the West Indies in exchange for negroes. And in his report to the home government mentioned above, Cadillac complained of the selling of Indian slaves to the English by Bienville. Such transactions by the French officials were carried on secretly. The Sieur de Ste. Heleine, nephew of Bienville, was killed by the English allied Indians while on such an expedition to sell Indians to the English of Carolina.

Some opposition to the trade was shown by the Jesuits, since the hoped for result of having numbers of slaves to convert, if purchased by the French, did not materialize. Accordingly, in 1693, they petitioned the governor of Canada to prohibit the trade in Indian slaves. The request was granted and an order issued to that effect, but without definite result. The "coureurs de bois" continued the trade in spite of the penalty of fine and imprisonment.

Certain of the Indians possessed by the explorers were gifts from Indian chiefs. On his second voyage, in 1535, the chiefs of the Saguenay River country gave Cartier three children. Afterwards, owing to mutual suspicions on the part of the French and Indians, one of these children made her escape. On the resumption of good feeling, the Indians promised to return her. Later, another chief offered Cartier two children, one of whom was accepted.

In 1564, Laudonnière led an expedition to the region of Florida. Desiring to penetrate into the interior and realizing that the friendship of the Indians was necessary for such an attempt, he sought to obtain from an Indian chief two of his prisoners, whom he proposed to use in winning the friendship of another chief by presenting them to him. At first, the chief declined to give away the prisoners; but, upon Laudonnière's renewing his request, the chief yielded, the prisoners were produced, and were taken back by the French to Fort Carolina.

Champlain desired to send to France some girls to have them "instructed in the law of God and good manners." An opportunity to satisfy this desire came with the wish of the Montagnais to present something to the French traveler. Three girls were given him, whom he named Faith, Hope and Charity, and whom he had instructed in religion, domestic work, etc. Still other Indians were taken to France by the expedition. One of the sagamores of the Montagnais gave his son to M. du Pont for that purpose. Still another savage, an Iroquois woman, the Frenchman begged of the tribe which was about to eat her. Other and similar instances of obtaining Indians are recorded for the same general humanitarian and religious purpose.

The Illinois gave Marquette and Jolliet an Indian slave boy, whom Jolliet took with him when going to Quebec and who was drowned on the journey. The Ottawa gave Marquette a young man, and a Kishkakon chief gave him "a little slave he had brought from the Illinois a few months before." In the same manner, Indians were given to La Salle and to his companion, Tonti, on their expeditions. In 1699, Father Anastasius accepted from the Indians the gift of an Indian girl as a slave. In 1703, M. de Saint Cosmé, a missionary priest traveling from Canada to Natchez, possessed in his party a young Indian slave boy.

When Du Lhut was in Montreal in 1678, the savages gave him three slaves. At another time, 1684, the Indians wished to give him some slaves as an atonement for their having murdered some Frenchmen. In 1700, the "Mantantons" (Mdewakanton), at a feast in his honor, presented Le Sueur, among other gifts, with an Indian slave. In 1719, La Harpe, on his journey northwest from Natchitoches, was given a young Kansas slave by the chiefs of several nations gathered together. One of the chiefs expressed his sorrow that he had but one slave to give, and La Harpe, in his letter to Terrisse, regrets that he did not arrive sooner, and by receiving them as slaves, prevent the seventeen companions of his slave from being eaten.

The Indians realized that the trade in captive slaves was profitable. When, in 1724, the Kansas tribe charged de Bourgmont double price for slaves sold him, they feared that he would be angry at the price asked, and that in consequence they would lose future trade. So they presented him with five slaves as a gift.

Throughout history the children of slave mothers have generally been considered slaves. A report on the condition of Louisiana, 1716, declared that the inhabitants were accustomed to sell the children of their Indian female slaves. Later, in 1724, a royal decree provided that children born of marriages between slaves should be slaves, and should belong to the masters of their mothers, and not to the masters of their fathers, if father and mother should belong to different masters.

The uses to which Indian slaves were put, either in early or later colonial times, were determined by economic conditions. Among the explorers, the need for guides and interpreters was imperative, and one finds the French, like the Spanish, using Indian slaves for this purpose. On his second expedition, Cartier made such use of the Indian children whom he carried to France on his first expedition. Laudonnière, in 1564, intended to use slaves for this purpose. Du Lhut purchased a slave to act as guide. The Mallet expedition, in 1739, used a slave as guide. One of the slaves purchased by de Bourgmont on his expedition in 1724, was retained with the expedition as interpreter, and was taught French by de Bourgmont himself. Doubtless the instances might be multiplied if the records were complete, though it is not likely that enslaved Indians were used for this purpose to the same extent as the friendly allied or converted Indians.

The French never sent out any great expeditions like those of the Spaniards. Hence among the explorers the use of slaves as domestics was limited. Among the colonists, one finds Le Page du Pratz, on his arrival in Louisiana, buying an Indian woman to act as cook and interpreter. The early Louisiana colonists experienced the need for servants, and, May 26, 1700, expressed the hope that the Indians would supply such need. The life of the Illinois colonist was less luxurious than that of the inhabitant of Louisiana; in consequence, the need of slaves in household service was less.

Early in the eighteenth century life among the French of Louisiana, both rich and poor, was quite licentious, and one of the means of fostering this life was the use of Indian women, slave and free. The demoralization resulting from such a condition attracted attention, and in 1709 it was urged that girls suitable for wives be sent over in order "to prevent these disorders and debaucheries."

Agricultural pursuits appear to have been the chief labor to which the French put Indian slaves. Such pursuits, along with trading, formed the chief industry of the colonies. But it was the general tendency of the French to prefer the novelty and excitement of the trader's life, rather than the more quiet existence of the agriculturalist. Bienville complained much of this state of affairs, and sought to remedy it. The consequence of this tendency was to make the price of labor high, and the use of Indian slaves was a means at hand to solve the difficulty. In the simpler life of the inhabitants of the Illinois country, agriculture was the chief industry of the settlers until the close of the period under discussion. And the farmers increased the results of their industry by the extensive use of Indian slaves.

Throughout the French territory in the military stations, both soldiers and frontiersmen found use for their Indian women slaves as cooks and in performing the other domestic labors of fort and camp.

The male slaves were used in erecting fortifications, performing other heavy labor, and as guides in military expeditions.

The custom of using Indian slaves as a bribe or reward was common. In either case the purpose of the whites was the same: to procure the friendship and alliance of the tribes. In the northwest the French demanded that certain subdued tribes bring them Indian slaves, which they might use to replace the members of the allied tribes whom the conquered tribes had killed during the war. In the area where the claims of the European nations overlapped, alliance of the tribes was especially desired by each nation. These Indian captive slaves or slaves purchased from other tribes were often returned to their own tribes as a peace offering or as a token of friendship. Thus the alliance of the tribes was won, and a barrier created against the encroachments of the Spanish and the English. Such use was made of slaves by de Bourgmont, in 1724, in the Kansas country. With a messenger sent from there to the Comanche, he sent also two Comanche slaves whom he purchased from the Kansas in order that his messenger be well received. He also purchased some Padouca slaves in order to return them to their people.

In 1728, the king of France issued an edict regarding certain concessions of land, and required a tax of five livres on each slave, the proceeds of which were to be used in building churches and hospitals. Thus the Indian slaves, along with the negroes, served as a property basis in this one instance, as they did many times in the English colonies. They were also regarded as property in all legal and business transactions and were classed along with negroes, domestic animals and real estate, which could be sold to satisfy their owners' debts.

The early slavery among the French was mild in nature. The system was of a patriarchal type. The Indian slaves often worked along with their owners, especially those engaged in agricultural labor, and were treated as children who must be guided, directed, punished or rewarded by their superiors. Cramoisy, writing of Bienville's expedition of 1737, states that a Chickasaw slave who acted as guide, had belonged to his owner five years and was always treated as one of the family. A French settler in the Fox Valley is spoken of as living with his Pawnee slaves in feudal style.

The relation of the French and the Indians, bond or free, was always different from that existing between the English and the Indians. The Frenchman never looked upon the Indians with the disdain and contempt for an inferior race which was displayed by the English. Marriage between French and Indians was common. The social result of this close connection was more pronounced in case of the Frenchman than in that of the Indian. It meant the "Indianizing" of the Frenchman, or the bringing him to the social level and to the life and habits of the red man. The most striking result of this tendency was supplied by the "coureur de bois;" but the same result was apparent even in the case of the superior colonists of lower Louisiana. And to this result the Indian slave contributed in a measure. The lack of social distinction between Frenchman and native tended toward kind treatment on the part of the owner, and to a shifting of the social planes of master and slave toward that of equality. Yet instances of cruelty to slaves are not lacking. The punishments of the age were cruel, whether the offender was bond or free.

It has been said that the dominating feature of French colonial life was trade. But religious and commercial advancement went hand in hand. From the earliest arrival of the French, the missionary labors of the Church extended not only to the Indian tribes, but also to the negro and Indian slaves held by the colonists. The conversion of the Indian was an asset for the growth of trade. French commissions, as well as Spanish, provided for the conversion of the Indians. Priest and friar were everywhere present. Each Christianized Indian slave marked a gain in the advancement of the faith, and made possible a readier access to trade with the convert's tribe and those of his friends. But the religious training and teaching of slaves were not entirely a matter of policy. It was rather a part of the generally kind treatment of the master. The rites of the Church were commonly accorded them. The Louisiana church records certain accounts of the birth, baptism, marriage and burial of Indian slaves. The Mobile and New Orleans registers are similar to the church registers to be found throughout Lower Canada wherever a church was established. The parish registers of Levis, Quebec and Long Point are cases in point. Throughout the first and part of the second half of the eighteenth century, these registers show that Indian slaves, many of whom, in

Quebec for instance, were brought from Louisiana, were baptized, and then records kept of such baptisms as in the case of the whites. The church records of Kaskaskia and Vincennes make frequent mention of the birth, baptism and death of Indian slaves (called Panis) down to the time of British occupation; but from that time they became more and more infrequent as Indian slavery gradually gave way to negro slavery. The baptismal register of Mobile, Alabama, dating from 1704 to 1740, contains baptismal records of whites, blacks and Indians. From the register it appears that witnesses to the baptism of a slave were not considered necessary, though sometimes used. In some instances the person baptized is recorded as the slave of a certain person. In other cases he is mentioned as a slave, and the owner's name is not given. The earliest baptism of an Indian slave in this record is that of a fifteen-year-old slave of Iberville. Baptisms of Indian slaves are quite as frequent as those of negro slaves. February 8, 1734, is the latest date of Indian slave baptisms in the register. Some of these Indian slaves are recorded as legitimate children of slave parents.

The laws of France did not permit the holding of any Christian in slavery. This meant that the conversion of Indians or other slaves would confer freedom upon them. But the law was never enforced. The French clergy went on continuously with their work of converting, baptizing and teaching both bond and free; and in the "Code Noir" of 1724, Louis XV commanded that all slaves in the French colonies, "be educated in the Apostolic Roman Catholic religion, and be baptized," and enjoined their owners to have these matters attended to within a reasonable time. The code dealt directly with negro slaves, but the Indian slaves still in existence were necessarily included in its provisions.

In Louisiana Indian slavery began with the founding of the colony. A report of the colony written in 1704, states that at Fort Louis de Louisiane, having a white population of 180 soldiers and 27 French families numbering 64 persons, (a total of 244 white persons), there were six Indian boy slaves from twelve to eighteen years of age, and five Indian girl slaves from fifteen to twenty years of age. In 1708, the colony consisted of fourteen officers, seventy-six soldiers, thirteen sailors, three priests, six mechanics, one Indian interpreter, twenty-four laborers, twenty-eight women, twenty-five children, (a total of 190 free persons), and eighty Indian slaves. In 1713, besides the soldiers, there were twenty-eight families, twenty negroes and a few Indian women and children. The following statistics are given in the archives of the Ministry of the Colonies in Paris:

Census of New Orleans, November 24, 1721. Recapitulation: Men, 446; Women, 140; Children, 96; Negro slaves, 523; Indian slaves, 51. Census of New Orleans in 1723. Recapitulation: Men, bearing arms, 229; Women or girls, 169; Children, 183; Orphans, 45; Slaves, 267. General census of the Colony of Louisiana on January 1, 1726. Recapitulation: Masters, 1952; Hired men and servants, 276; Negro slaves, 1540; Indian slaves, 229. General census of the Department of New Orleans on July 1, 1727. Recapitulation:

	Masters	Hired	Negroes	Savage
New Orleans	729	65	127	17
The Bayou and Chantilly	42	5	73	5
Inhabitants up the River on the Right	243	26	883	45
Idem on the Left	306	35	456	5
On the Shore of Lake Ponchartrain..	7	2	14	
On Bayou Tauchpao	2	5	8	1
Total	1329	138	1561	73

From these statistics it will be seen that in Louisiana the negro slaves far outnumbered the Indian slaves, and that the ratio of the number of Indian slaves to the number of whites in the colony was very small. A memoir concerning Natchitoches, 1720 or 1721, states that the number of black slaves in that settlement was thirty-four, and the number of Indian slaves, six (two men and four women). A report on the condition of Louisiana at large in 1744 declared that there were very few Indian slaves in the colony, "because we are at peace with all nations: these we have were taken in former wars, and we keep them." Another account, in 1750, states that the inhabitants of New Orleans consist of "French, Negroes, and some savages who are slaves—all these together do not number . . . more than 1,200 persons."

The smallness of the number of Indian slaves in Louisiana appears due to several reasons: the generally friendly relations of the

French and the neighboring tribes; the absence of extensive agriculture at an early date; the neglect of the colonial authorities to develop a trade in savage slaves, like that of Carolina; and the rapid increase in the importation of negro slaves by the time that occupations profitable for slave labor were developed.

In the northern part of the Mississippi Valley, also, Indian slavery began with the coming of the whites. Slavery at Vincennes and in the country below the present site of Terre Haute, Indiana, was regulated by the laws of Louisiana. That in the country to the north was regulated by the customs of Canada. Indian slavery in Canada began early. Record exists of Indian slaves in Montreal in 1670. In Louisiana the greater number of slaves were negroes; whereas in Canada the larger portion were Indians. In the early history of Vincennes most of the slaves were Indians, for the inhabitants were more extensively engaged in the Indian trade than in agricultural pursuits. The same was true of the country about Detroit. Some of these Indians went, of course, to Louisiana; but the larger portion went to Canada. A report in 1750 shows that in the five French villages of the Illinois country there were eleven hundred whites, three hundred blacks and sixty Indian slaves. Indian slavery, already giving way to negro slavery, continued so to do after British occupation.

Indian slaves, mostly children, are recorded in Detroit in 1710, 1712, and 1715. Their use continued there until the English occupation. A report in 1733 shows the Canadians trading in Indian slaves whom they seized or purchased from other Indians. By the terms of the surrender of Montreal, 1760, already mentioned, the English guaranteed to the settlers all the rights in property they had enjoyed, and Article IV of the capitulation provided that all negro and Pawnee slaves should remain in their condition of servitudes. In 1763, the population of Canada comprised about 70,000 Europeans, 30,000 Indians and 400 black slaves. It will be seen that the number of negro slaves was very small as compared with the number in Louisiana. And, judging from the frequent mention of Indian slaves in the parish records, and the not inconsiderable trade in such slaves that went on with the western tribes, one may concede the truth of the assertion that the number of Indian slaves in that territory, under Canadian law, exceeded the number of negro slaves, even though, in proportion to the white population, the number was small.

In the French colonies, the earliest method of manumission was to grant slaves their freedom verbally and without further formality. In the Wisconsin country, during the first half of the eighteenth century, at least, there appears to have been some requirement or obligation, perhaps imposed by custom, for the owners of Indian slaves to free them after a certain period of servitude. But on April 11, 1735, a memorandum of the king to de Beauharnois and Hocquart declared that the judges of the colonies might conform themselves to the custom of considering the Indians held in servitude as slaves, and that masters who might wish to grant such Indians their freedom should do so by notarial deed. Accordingly, on September 1, 1736, an ordinance was issued at Quebec by Hocquart, the intendant, stating, with the consent of the Marquis de Beauharnois, governor and lieutenant-general of the colony, that anyone wishing to free any slave must make affirmation to that effect before a notary, to which he would be held. The act would be registered in the "greffe" of the nearest royal jurisdiction. A manumission performed in any other way was declared null and void.

As above stated, it was customary for the French colonists to sell the children of their female slaves. The practice might, and did, mean that a father sold his own child. Notice of the matter having been called to the attention of the king, an attempt was made to prevent the practice by inserting in the instructions sent to the colony in 1721-1722, a provison forbidding the sale of either a female negro or Indian slave or her child, if a free colonist were the father of such a child. The same instructions further declared it in harmony with religion and the welfare of the colony that at the end of a certain period of time both mother and child should be given their liberty, and so be made free inhabitants of the colony. Such a kindly attitude on the part of the home government met with but little response in the colonies.

Several causes contributed to the passing of Indian slavery in French territory. Wherever the American Indians have been brought into contact with the white races, the result has been disaster to the red men. The Indian's nature is not adapted to the white man's scheme of life. The Indian absorbed the white man's diseases and vices. Not the least of these vices was the love for strong drink, and the weakness of the natives in this respect was recognized and encouraged by the traders of all nations. The decrease in game and other food supplies as the Indians retreated from the sea, famine followed by gluttonous excesses, wasting of the forests of the table lands, all resulted in inferior living conditions and a consequent decrease in the birth rate and weakening of the tribes. As the weakened tribes withdrew from contact with the whites they usually joined with stronger tribes. The removal of tribes from their immediate neighborhood, and the union with other and distant tribes, acted as a check on the whites' obtaining Indians as slaves. Such was the case with the tribes from whom the French of the Illinois country and Canada drew their slaves.

It has already been seen that the French missionaries of early colonial days believed that the enslavement of Indians would serve as a means of spreading the Christian religion. They found, however, that the method of obtaining Indian slaves by trade only increased the distribution of spirituous liquors among the tribes; and so, in 1693, they asked the king to prohibit the Indian slave trade. An order to this effect was accordingly issued, but with little result. The "coureurs de bois" found means to carry on the trade clandestinely notwithstanding the penalty attached. Again, in 1736, the king decided formally to prohibit the enslavement of Indians and issued a decree to that effect; but to no advantage.

The gradual passing out of existence of Indian slavery, furthermore, was due, in no small measure, to its unsatisfactory character. The leading colonists early made up their minds to this effect. Bienville, in a letter to the Minister of Marine, July 28, 1706, stated that the French colonists earnestly requested negroes to till their lands, for whom they were willing to pay silver, since the colonies found Indian slaves unsatisfactory. He furthermore requested permission for the colonists to transport Indian slaves to the West Indian Islands in exchange for negroes. The fact that the colonists were willing to trade three Indians for two negroes is sufficient proof of the small value of Indians as slaves. Another letter to the home government, in 1717, records the same state of affairs in the colony.

Indian slaves were prone to run away, and their use by the French as individual laborers, or their use only in small groups, if worked together, made escape comparatively easy. A letter of Périer to the home government, May 12, 1728, declared that the traffic in Indian slaves and their use in the French colony was contrary to the welfare of the country, since such slaves served but a short time before they escaped back to their own tribes or to neighboring Indians. Moreover, these deserting Indians persuaded the negro slaves to run away with them. A letter from the President of the Navy Board to la Jonquière and Bigot, May 4, 1749, represented that the Indian slaves brought up in the colony by the officers or by the inhabitants, generally left them when they attained a certain age and again became uncivilized; that they were the more dangerous on account of the knowledge which they had acquired of the country, being better able than others to make incursions therein; and that through the habit of keeping these slaves the whites were dissuaded from becoming domestic servants.

Among the slaves the boys were not so much to be depended upon as the girls, since they were stubborn, resented more strongly their being held in slavery, and were more inclined to run away. Long's Journal, 1768-1782, speaking of the western Indians, records: "They are also full of pride and resentment, and will not hesitate to kill their masters in order to gratify their revenge for a supposed injury. The girls are more docile, and assimilate much sooner into the manners of civilization." It is probable that slaves coming from the Pawnee tribe, and held so largely by the French of Detroit and Canada, were more satisfactory than those coming from other tribes. It has been said that it would be difficult to find another of the wild tribes of the continent capable of subjection to domestic slavery. But the Pawnee, like other slaves, ran away.

Though Indian slaves were not as profitable laborers as might be desired, their loss was to be avoided, if possible. The matter was so serious as to interest the action of the authorities, and in 1709, Jacques Raudot, intendant of Canada, issued an ordinance containing an injunction which forbade any slave running away, and containing provisions for imposing a fine of fifty livres on those who aided such runaways.

Indian slaves were too few in number and too inferior in capacity for labor to supply the needs of the colonists. So an attempt was made by the home government to supply the needed laborers by establishing the system of indentured servants in the colonies. On November 16, 1716, an ordinance directed that vessels leaving France for any of the king's American colonies were to carry thither, if of fifty tons, three servants; of sixty to one hundred tons, four servants; of one hundred tons and upward, six servants. The period of service of such servants was fixed at three years. They were required to be of sound body, between the ages of eighteen and forty, and in height not under four feet. These servants were to be examined before the officers of the admiralty to see if they fulfilled the requirements of the law, and were to receive another examination by the commissary on landing in America. Such of the redemptioners as the captain might not sell were to be given to some of the planters who had none, and who were to pay their passage. The ordinance was repeated May 20, 1721, with the additional provision that merchants of the ports having permission to trade with the colonies were to pay sixty livres for each redemptioner whom they had to furnish, if individuals for that purpose were not furnished them by the government.

The purpose of France, in making such careful provision for sending indentured servants to the New World, was a real effort to increase the population and, therefore, the trade of America. Moreover, the home government feared the danger that might come to the colony by the increase of the black over the white population, and hoped this indentured servant system would be a means to that end. But the scheme had little result. The colonists preferred black slaves to white servants. Their term of service was for life instead of a short period. They were easier to control, cheaper to keep, and were better workers. Yet, it has been estimated that from 1711 to 1728, two thousand five hundred redemptioners were brought to the French colonies. Such a number of white servants must, in a measure, have checked the acquisition of Indian slaves.

But the need for laborers was to be supplied in the French colonies by the black, instead of the white race. Although the home government grew to fear the result of the rapid increase of the negro element, yet, at first, it favored the importation of blacks to the American colonies. In 1688, Louis XIV issued an edict authorizing the importation of negroes from Africa into America. Article XIV of the letters patent granted by the king to Crozat, September 30, 1712, gave the latter permission, if he found it advisable to have the blacks in Louisiana, to send a ship every year to the coast of Guinea to obtain them, and to sell them to the inhabitants of the colony. So, from the first, negro slaves were present in the French colonies, though during the earlier part of the eighteenth century, they were outnumbered by the Indian slaves.

In 1713, there were but twenty negro slaves in Louisiana, but with the granting of the charter of the Western Company in 1717, their increased importation began. A provision of the charter required that during the lifetime of the charter (twenty-five years,) not less than three thousand negroes be carried to the colony. The first large importation was made by the Company in June, 1719, when five hundred negroes were brought from the coast of Guinea. For several years, the importation of negroes into Louisiana was one of the most profitable monopolies of the Western Company. One authority states that, during the period from 1717 to 1723, one thousand, four hundred and forty-one negroes were brought in. Another states that from 1717 to 1728 eighteen were introduced. The "Code Noir" of 1724 shows that the negro slaves had become the majority by that time, for no direct mention is made in it to Indian slaves. In 1727, it was reported that on each of the "concessions," or leading grants, there were, at least, sixty negroes cultivating corn, rice, indigo and tobacco.

To open up and work the mineral resources of Louisiana, Philip François Renault was sent out by the Company of the West in 1719. On his way, he bought at San Domingo, in the name of his Company, five hundred negroes for working the mines. These negroes were taken into the Illinois country. The number of negroes in the Illinois country never equaled that of the country farther south, yet in 1750, a Jesuit missionary found one thousand, one hundred whites, three hundred blacks, and sixty Indian slaves in five villages of the Illinois country, and by 1763, the black population numbered over nine hundred.

From the foregoing account it will be seen that the steadily increasing number of negro slaves, resulting from a promotion of the commercial interests of the home government and from the more satisfactory labor performed by the blacks, must have been the leading cause that produced the steady decrease in the number of Indian slaves among the French.

INDIAN SLAVERY

PART II. THE INSTITUTION AS PRACTICED BY THE ENGLISH

CHAPTER IV. THE NUMBER OF INDIAN SLAVES

To arrive at any knowledge of the exact number of Indian slaves in any of the English colonies is impossible. Census reports and other vital statistics are infrequent or lacking, especially in the early colonial period; and often in such statistics as are extant Indian slaves either receive no mention, or are classed with negro slaves without distinction. From existing records, however, one is able to obtain a knowledge of the comparative numbers in the different groups of colonies, and to some extent in the individual colonies, during the colonial period. New England and the southern colonies were the sections that employed Indian slave labor most extensively, the south taking precedence, for climatic conditions there were more favorable, and economic conditions made necessary a larger quantity of servile labor than was required in the north. Yet New England made use of the natives as slaves as long as they lasted, and drew further supplies from Maine, the Carolinas, and other districts.

Among the English colonies, the Carolinas stood first in the use of Indians as slaves. Such use began with the founding of the colony. The need for laborers was great; the source of supply was near at hand and the colonists availed themselves of their opportunity. Probably captives of the Stono War became the Indian slaves mentioned in the inventory of Captain Valentine Byrd, "one of the grandees of the time." In a report on conditions in the colony, made to the proprietors, September 17, 1708, by Governor Nathaniel Johnson and his council, the number of Indian men slaves was given as 500, Indian women slaves, as 600, Indian children slaves, as 300, a total of 1400 Indian slaves. The number of negroes at the same time was stated as 4100, of indentured servants, 120, and of free whites, 3960. The governor gave the cause of the rapid increase in the number of the Indian slaves during the five preceding years, as "our late conquest over the French and Spanish, and the success of our forces against the Appalaskys and in other Indian engagements."

Only a small portion of the whole number of Indians enslaved were kept in the colony. Yet, in 1708, it was estimated that the native population furnished one-fourth of the whole number of slaves in South Carolina. The public records of that colony contain a list of ninety-eight Indian slaves with their owners' names, taken by the Spaniards and their allies in 1715, during the Indian war, and carried to St. Augustine. The number of these slaves belonging to individual persons varied from one to ten. A report of 1723 mentions the number of slaves in South Carolina and Georgia as ranging from 16,000 to 20,000, "chiefly negroes and a few Indians."

Another report of the following year estimates the number of slaves as 32,000, "mostly negroes". "In 1728, the population of St. Thomas' parish, South Carolina, consisted of 565 whites, 950 negro slaves, and 60 Indian slaves." From these statistics, it will be seen that the number of Indian slaves was much smaller than the number of negroes, and that it was growing smaller toward the middle of the eighteenth century, while that of negroes was constantly increasing.

The early history of Indian slavery in Georgia is so bound up with that of Carolina, the Indian wars, and the difficulties with the Spaniards of Florida, as to require but little especial attention. After the settlement of Georgia as a separate colony, occasional mention is made of Indian slaves. In 1759, as the basis for a tax bill, the number of slaves was placed at 2500, but a committee of the legislature declared the number to have been underestimated. How many of this number were Indians is not known. The colony was settled at a time when Indian slavery was passing out of existence. So it is safe to state that the number of such slaves was small.

The number of Indian slaves in Virginia, also, was small, owing largely to the number of indentured servants, and to the early introduction and fitness of the negroes for the labor of the colony. In 1671, Berkeley reported the whole population of the colony as 40,000, the number of indentured servants as 6000, and that of slaves as 2000. But no division of slaves according to color was made. In certain sections but few slaves were used. The Scotch-Irish and the Germans preferred their own labor to that of slaves. Some Indians were taken in war, but they were inconsiderable when compared with the number captured in the Carolinas. Occasional mention of Indian slaves is found well into the eighteenth century.

Indian slavery in Massachusetts began early. Following the Pequot War, 1637, forty-eight captives were retained as slaves in the colony. After King Philip's War, 1675, also, certain of the captives were made slaves, but no record exists of the exact number. The various records and histories of the Massachusetts towns show a general distribution of Indian slaves throughout the colony during the colonial period, such as existed following the two Indian wars above noted. Mere mention may be made of some of these: Plymouth, Boston, Roxbury, Ipswich, Quincy, Charleston, Malden, Haverhill, Milton. None of the official reports on the condition of New England makes mention of Indian slaves. But statistics show the number of slaves in Massachusetts in 1720 to have been 2000, including a few Indians. In 1790, according to the United States census report, the number of slaves in the state was 6,001, which number included about 200 half breed Indians. Since Massachusetts took the lead in the two Indian wars of New England, it seems likely that the number of Indian slaves in that colony exceeded that in either Connecticut or Rhode Island.

The Rhode Island laws from 1636 to 1704 make no mention of Indian slaves. Yet they were held in the colony before 1704. The records of Block Island show them there in sufficient numbers, in 1675, to warrant the town council regulating their action. Captives taken in King Philip's War were retained in the colony temporarily as slaves. The Boston newspapers occasionally mention runaway Indian slaves of Block Island. Both negro and Indian slavery reached a development in colonial Narragansett unusual in the northern colonies. In 1730, South Kingston had a population of 935 whites, 333 negroes, and 223 Indian slaves. Eighteen years later, the proportion of races was nearly the same: 1405 whites, 380 negroes, and 193 Indians. As late as 1778, the laws of Rhode Island mentioned Indian slaves.

Indian slavery in Connecticut began almost with the founding of the colony, and came about as a result of the Pequot War (1636). The captives taken in the war were assigned directly to the colony and were retained and distributed among the inhabitants. The colonists appear to have held a greater number of such slaves then than at any later period. Certain Indians, also, were kept in the colony as slaves following King Philip's War, but the number is unknown. Local histories show them in different towns well into the eighteenth century. An answer sent to a query from the Board of Trade in 1680 states that there were then thirty slaves in Connecticut, but no mention is made of Indian slaves though they existed in the colony.

The number of Indian slaves in New Hampshire was undoubtedly very small. During the Pequot War and King Philip's War, New Hampshire remained at peace with the Indians, and the statement has been made that no New Hampshire merchant or captain, during the Indian wars, kidnapped natives or consciously broke faith with them. The close connection with Massachusetts, however, made inevitable the existence of Indian slaves in the former colony, and the Boston newspapers occasionally mention such slaves as late as approximately 1750.

In the middle group of colonies, the number of Indian slaves was never large, and, in comparison with that in either the southern or New England groups, it was conspicuously small. There appear to have been more of such slaves in New York than in any other colony of the group, a condition due to its greater trade with the colonies which exported them. The English colony, furthermore, took over no Indian slaves from its Dutch predecessor.

The inhabitants of New York, under Dutch or English rule, never waged any war on the order of those in New England against the Indian tribes. Nor did the distribution of New England captives affect this colony to any great extent. A few Indian slaves were introduced from foreign parts, but the selling and holding of Indians as slaves was never a general custom. The existence of Indian slaves, however, was recognized by a decree of the governor and council in 1680. An Indian slave was sold, July 30, 1687, in Hempstead, Long Island. The narrative of grievances against Jacob Leisler includes the following: "The same night, December 23, 1689, an Indian slave, belonging to Philip French, was dragged to the Fort (New York), and there imprisoned." Aaron Schuyler of New York, 1693, gave to each of his two daughters, in his will, an Indian slave woman. In July, 1703, the governor received a petition regarding an Indian slave. The will of William Smith, of the manor of St. George, Suffolk County, April 23, 1704, divided a number of negro and Indian slaves among his children. In 1715, certain Indians complained that the whites were enslaving native children entrusted to them for instruction. In 1724, the Reverend Mr. Jenny reported: "There are a few negro and Indian slaves in my parish." On July 3, 1726, the Reverend Mr. Vesey of New York, in a letter to the Society for the Propagation of the Gospel in Foreign Parts, stated that in the colony there were "about one thousand and four hundred Indian and negro slaves," but tells nothing about the proportion of each. Colonel Johnson's letter to Governor Clinton, January 22, 1750, and William Johnson's letter to G. W. Banyar, June 28, 1771, the former relating to Indian children held as slaves, and the latter mentioning a Pawnee Indian slave in New York, show the existence of such slaves until a late date. Occasional mention is found in the newspapers of the time of runaway Indian slaves. From the evidence the conclusion is that although the existence of Indian slavery was continuous in New York throughout the colonial period, the number of Indian slaves, in comparison with that of individual colonies in New England and the south, was small.

William Penn, speaking of his purpose in founding a colony in America said: "I went thither to lay the foundation of a free colony for all mankind." Yet in Pennsylvania existed the indentured servant, the negro slave and the Indian slave. Considering the attitude and the relations of Penn and his followers toward the red men, one would hardly expect to find the Indians enslaved. In the absence of wars with the natives, no Indian captives were reduced to servitude. The Indian slaves used were brought from other colonies. The newspapers contain accounts of their being bought and sold, and of their running away, as in the other colonies. The leading men of the colony owned them. Penn's own deputy, Governor William Markham, owned one, born in 1700, who, by the terms of Markham's will, was to be freed at the age of twenty-five. In a bill of sale of the personal effects of Sir William Keith, dated May 26, 1726, an Indian woman and her son were mentioned among the seventeen slaves listed.

In 1780, a farmer of East Nottingham, Chester County, registered, at the county seat, the names of an Indian girl. aged twenty-four years, a slave for life, and of an Indian man in slavery until he arrived at the age of thirty-one years. The action of the

Friends' Yearly Meeting in, also, shows that Indian slaves, as well as negro slaves, were owned by the members of that religious society.

It has been said that slavery in New Jersey was more prevalent among the Dutch settlements and the plantations of South Jersey than in the Calvinistic towns of East Jersey. Since the number of negro slaves throughout the Dutch possessions of America was considerable, it may be concluded that the scarcity of Indian slaves was due to conditions rather than to scruples, though the presence of a Quaker element may have affected the situation. The proximity of the powerful Iroquois, also, by shutting off the source of possible supply, may have had something to do with the matter. The number of Indian slaves in New Jersey was very small, yet the newspapers of the time show the presence of such a servile class in the colony throughout the colonial period.

In Maryland, there appears to have been even a smaller number of Indian slaves than in New Jersey. There were no Indian wars to furnish captives, and the Indians from the Carolinas were sent to ports in New England where the demand for them was greater. In Maryland indentured servants largely supplied the need for laborers and so minimized the use of the natives as slaves.

CHAPTER V. PROCESSES OF ENSLAVEMENT: WARFARE

OF the processes in vogue among the English for the acquisition of Indian slaves, the most productive was that of warfare. With the exception of the Pequot War and King Philip's War in New England, the Indian wars in the English colonies were confined to the south, and there the greatest number of Indian war captives were enslaved.

After the Indian massacre of 1622 in Virginia, there was published in London, in the same year, a tract entitled: *"The Relation of the Barbarous Massacre in Time of Peace and League, treacherously executed by the native infidels upon the English, the Twenty-second of March, 1622, published by Authority."* The general trend of the tract is to show the good that might result to the plantation from this disaster. Number five of the possible results reads: "Because the Indians, who before were used as friends, may now most justly be compelled to servitude in mines, and the like, of whom some may be sent for the use of the Summer Islands."

The policy advocated by the tract was carried out in succeeding Indian wars in Virginia. The accounts of a certain Thomas Smallcomb, lieutenant at Fort Royal on Pamunkey, who was probably killed in the war with Opechancanough, show him possessed at the time of his death, 1646, of several Indian slaves. It seems probable that these slaves were captives in war. After his rebellion, 1676, Bacon sold some of his Indian prisoners. The rest were disposed of by Governor Berkeley.

From the beginning of the colony, the settlers of Carolina were in trouble with the Indians. In September, 1671, war was declared against the Kussoe, a tribe on the southern frontier who posed as allies of the Spaniards, and who vexed the Carolina settlers with petty depredations. The Kussoe were quickly defeated, and the prisoners sent to be sold out of the colony, unless ransomed by their countrymen. During the war with the Stono Indians in 1680, the captive Indians were brought to Charleston and sold by Governor West to the traders in the colony to be carried to the West Indies as slaves.

The breaking out of the war of the Spanish Succession in 1701 gave Governor Moore a chance to attack the Spanish Indians, capture and sell them under the excuse of the rules of war. Therefore, in 1702, he led a force of militia and Indians against St. Augustine, burned the city, and carried off, as slaves, whatever Indians he could obtain from the Spanish Indian villages along the way. A second attack on St. Augustine was made by Moore in 1704, with the purpose of destroying missions and carrying off slaves. An advance into the territories of the Apalachee resulted in the destruction of several missions, and the capture of more than a thousand Indians, some free, some slave. Nearly all the Apalachee were distributed as slaves among the Carolina settlers. The enslavement of Indians, indeed, was carried on wholesale. A letter to the proprietors, July 10, 1708, states that "the garrison of St. Augustine is by this war reduced to the bare walls, their cattle and Indian towns all consumed, either by us in our invasion of that place, or by our Indian subjects . . . they have driven the Floridians to the islands of the cape, have brought in and sold many hundred of them, and maybe now continue that trade, so that in some five years, they'll reduce the barbarians to a fearless number." In 1708, Colonel Barnwell of South Carolina made an expedition to the Appalachian province of Florida. It is thought that this was the time when Captain Nairn of South Carolina, with a party of Yamasee Indians, advanced to the vicinity of Lake Okechobee and brought back a number of captive Indians as slaves. A similar expedition of Colonel Palmer in 1727 against the Yamasee resulted in the destruction of many Indian towns, the slaughter of many natives, and the carrying off of great numbers to Charleston as slaves.

As the result of the three expeditions sent by South Carolina from 1702 to 1708 against the Yamasee, Apalachee, and Timucua of northern Florida, there was carried back to Charleston, for sale as slaves, almost the entire population of seven towns, in all, some 1400 persons. The captives taken in 1715 when the Yamasee and Creek Indians made a foray upon the South Carolina frontier, were sold as slaves. Mr. Johnston, a South Carolina missionary of the Society for the Propagation of the Gospel in Foreign Parts, in his letter to the Society, December 19, 1715, states: "It is certain many of the Yammousees and Creek Indians were against the war all along. But our military men were so bent upon revenge, and so desirous to enrich themselves by making all the Indians slaves that fall into yr hands . .

. . that it is in vain to represent the cruelty and injustice of such a procedure."

Throughout the Tuscarora War in North Carolina, Indian captives were retained or sold as slaves. At the beginning of military operations, following the Indian massacre of 1711, the friendly Indians agreed to help the English against their enemy upon promise of a reward of six blankets for each man killed by them, and the usual price of slaves for each woman and child delivered as captives. During the course of the war several hundred Indian allies were used by the English, and these allies took advantage of the opportunity to obtain large number of Indian captives to sell to the slave traders of the time.

In an attack on an Indian fort in 1711, thirty-nine women and children were captured and disposed of in the settlements as slaves. The two chief expeditions during the war were those of Colonel Barnwell, who was sent by South Carolina in January, 1712, and of Colonel Moore in January and February, 1713. Colonel Barnwell's expedition took two hundred Indian women and children prisoners. The expedition of Colonel Moore virtually ended the war by capturing the fort in which the Tuscarora had taken refuge. Nine hundred men, women and children were killed or taken prisoners. In both expeditions the allied Indians secured as many as possible of the captured Indians whom they took along with them to sell as slaves in Charleston, and they still further increased their supply of slaves by attacking the peaceful Indians along the route of their return to South Carolina. During the course of the war more than seven hundred Indians were sold into slavery.

The earliest of the slave-producing wars in New England was that with the Pequot in 1637. The war consisted of two battles: the Mistick Fight, and the Swamp Fight. In the first of these two events, but seven captives were taken. In the second, the Swamp Fight, about one hundred and eighty captives were taken. Two of the sachems taken in the Swamp Fight were spared, on promise that they guide the English to the retreat of Sassacus. The other men captives, some twenty or thirty in number, were put to death. The remaining captives, consisting of about eighty women and children, were divided. Some were given to the soldiers, whether gratis or for pay does not appear.

Thirty were given to the Narraganset who were allies of the English, forty-eight were sent to Massachusetts and the remainder were assigned to Connecticut. The women and girls of the Massachusetts captives were distributed among the towns. It seems probable that Connecticut made a similar disposition of its share of the captives regardless of sex. The male children among the Massachusetts captives were ordered by the Massachusetts general court, 1637, to be carried to the Bermudas by William Pierce, and sold there as slaves. The shipload of Indians, however, consisting of fifteen boys and two women was taken by Captain Pierce to the West Indies. instead of to the Bermudas, and disposed of at the island of Providence. One Pequot seized near Block Island was sent to England.

It is possible that this single cargo of women and children was not the only one sent to the islands at this time. A letter from the Company of Providence Islands, replying from London, July 3, 1638, to letters from authorities on the island, and directing that special care be taken of the "cannibal negroes brought from New England," and a second letter written in 1639, when the company, fearing the danger that might arise from too large a number of negroes on the island, suggested that the negroes be sold or sent to New England or Virginia, may possibly have been called forth by a further purchase of Indians, or by an exchange of negroes for them.

By the time of King Philip's War, 1675-1676, the colonists were well accustomed to the sending of Indian captives out of the country, and to the use of them in their homes. The policy followed toward the Indians captured in this war was the same as that shown in the Pequot War. The captives were either exported for sale in the European or West Indian slave markets, or were retained in servitude in the colonies. In the beginning of the war, Captain Mosely captured eighty Indians, who were retained at Plymouth. In the following September, one hundred and seventy-eight were put on board a vessel commanded by Captain Sprague who sailed from Plymouth with them for Spain. In this same year, 1675, Indians, probably from the coast of Maine, were landed as slaves at Fayal, one of the Azores. Again in 1675, fifteen Indians were captured and sent to Boston, "tied neck to neck, like galley slaves." Much against the will of the populace they were given a trial. All were finally acquitted except two who were sentenced to be sold out of the country as slaves. During the years 1675 and 1676, one finds mention of the sale of Indians in Plymouth in groups of about a hundred, fifty-seven, three, one hundred and sixty, ten, and one. From June 25, 1675 to September 23, 1676, the records show the sale by the Plymouth colonial authorities of one hundred and eighty-eight Indians.

In the Massachusetts Bay colony a similar disposal of captives was accomplished. On one occasion about two hundred were transported and sold. There is extant a paper written by Daniel Gookin in 1676, one item of which is as follows: "a list of the Indian children that came in with John of Packachooge." The list shows twenty-one boys and eleven girls distributed throughout the colony.

With the close of the war after Philip's death, many of the Indian chiefs were executed at Boston and Plymouth, and most of the remaining chiefs with their captive followers were sold and shipped off as slaves outside the colonies. Those transported were carried to various parts: the Spanish West Indies, Spain, Portugal, Bermuda, Virginia, and the Azores.

Not all the Indians whose lives were spared were transported. Generally the men, rather than the women and children, were thus disposed of, though such was not always the case. One finds instances, like that of Philip's wife and son, when women and children were transported, and other instances when grown male Indians were retained in the colonies and sold to the colonists.

Not only were the Indians who themselves engaged in the war sold as slaves at home and abroad, but the wives and children of the captive males were also seized and consigned to slavery. In 1677, the Massachusetts general court ordered that the Indian children, boys and girls, whose parents had been in hostility with the colony or had lived among its enemies in the time of the war, and who were taken by force and given or sold to any of the inhabitants of the colony, should be at the disposal of their masters or their assignees. In the case of a certain Praying Indian, who withdrew from the English side and joined the Indian enemy, not only himself, but his wife and children were taken prisoners and held as slaves until redeemed by Eliot. The same policy was followed in Plymouth. A case in point is that of the chief, Popanooie, whose wife and children were retained in the colony as slaves, while he himself was transported and sold into slavery.

Both Plymouth and Massachusetts made a distinction between the children of those Indian enemies who were taken by force, and those who voluntarily gave themselves up to the colonial authorities. The children of the latter were to serve as slaves only until twenty-four years of age. The term of service of the former was not specified.

Neither Rhode Island nor Connecticut transported Indian slaves to the West Indies. Both colonies, however, retained Indian captives of King Philip's War, but only for limited periods of time, not for life. During the war numerous bands of the Indians surrendered to the English at Providence and Newport. The sentiment of the colony against enslaving Indians, here, as in Connecticut, the result of Quaker influence, had already been shown. So, in accordance with the spirit already expressed, it was voted by the town of Providence, August 14, 1676, to appoint a committee of five persons to dispose of the Indians there. The town agreed to abide by the action of the five men. The committee decided to sell the Indians in the colony for a term of years; one-half the proceeds of the sale to go to the captors, and the other half to the public treasury. The length of service was to depend upon the Indians' ages. Those under five years were to be simple bondsmen till thirty; all above five years, and under ten, till thirty-eight; above ten and under fifteen, till twenty-seven; above fifteen and under twenty, till twenty-six; such as were above thirty, seven years. Several receipts signed by this committee show that such sales occurred. A few days before, the Rhode Island companies had brought in forty-two Indian captives. These, and all other Indian prisoners held at the time, were sold into service in the colony for a period of nine years. The Indians thus sentenced did not become actual slaves according to the strictest interpretation of the term, since the persons who acquired them purchased only their services for a stated period of time, and not for life. Their condition is better explained by the term "involuntary indenture."

During King Philip's War Connecticut suffered nothing on its own soil from hostile Indians. In consequence the number of captive Indians enslaved was small, and only infrequent mention is found of these captives. A certain amount of the booty which the Connecticut troops assisted in taking fell to their lot, and among this booty were some of the captive Indians. An interesting record of such a slave is found in the account book of Major John Talcot (1674-1688) which includes his accounts as treasurer of the colony during King Philip's War. On opposite pages of the ledger occurs the following account (54-55): "1676. Captain John Stanton of Stonington, Dr., to Sundry Commissions given Captain Stanton to proceed against the Indians by which he gained much on the sale of captives." "Contra, 1677, April 30. Per received an Indian girl of him, about seven years old, which he gave me for commissions on the other side, or, at best, out of good will for any kindness to him."

In consequence of the small number of Indian captives enslaved in the colony, none was transported by colonial action. The privilege of thus getting rid of undesirable and troublesome Indian slaves by selling them out of the colony, was, however, conferred upon individual owners, when, May 10, 1677, the general court decreed: "for the prevention of those Indians running away, that are disposed in service by the Authority, that are of the enemy and have submitted to mercy, such Indians, if they be taken, shall be in the power of his master to dispose of him as a captive by transportation out of the country."

During the Indian wars in Virginia Governor Berkeley himself in a letter, 1668, to Robert Smith, militia commander in the Rappahannock country, not only proposed that, with the consent of the council of war, a war of extinction be waged against the northern Indians, but also suggested that the colonial government defray the expenses of the undertaking by the disposal of the women and children. Smith submitted Governor Berkeley's letter to the Rappahannock court for approval. In rendering their decision, the justices declared that the conduct of the northern Indians, notably the "Doagges" and the neighboring Indians, justified the taking of severe measures against them; and accordingly advised "with the assistance of Almighty God, by the strength of our northern part, utterly to eradicate [them], without further encroachment than the spoils of our enemies."

During Bacon's rebellion in 1676, the assembly at his instigation declared the enslavement of Indians for life to be legal, and made provision for granting captive Indians to soldiers as a partial inducement to volunteer. This act was repealed by the general act setting aside all the acts of this assembly that sat in 1676 under the rule of Bacon. But it was again revived by the assembly of 1679 called by Deputy-Governor Chicheley. Legal enslavement of Indians was prohibited by implication rather than by the terms of the act of 1691. But the North Carolina Indian troubles in November, 1711, once more brought the old law forward, and captive Indians belonging to tribes at war with the English were directed to be transported and sold, those capturing them to have the money of the sale.

It will be noted that, though in the case of Virginia, as in that of the other colonies, the disposal of the Indians captured in war was sanctioned by the colonial government, the action of the Virginia government in the matter ended with that sanction. By the acts of 1643 and 1658, the colony lost the right to possess servants. Therefore, the government during the Indian wars decreed that the captive Indians were the property of their captors who were entitled to the proceeds of their sale.

In the case of Maryland is found another colony in which the government intended that Indian captives taken in war should be sold for the benefit of the colony. At the time of the Puritan ascendency the Indians began to be troublesome. The Nanticoke of the Eastern shore began a war upon the settlers. March 29, 1652, on petition of the settlers, the general assembly attempted to pass a militia act. An expedition was planned, and a levy of troops made. The captive Indians were to be sold. But the government never had a chance to carry out any such sale, for the Puritans of Anne Arundel County refused to make their levies, and the expedition had to be abandoned.

During the Tuscarora War in North Carolina, one again finds an instance of a colonial government taking possession of the captive Indians, selling them as slaves, and depositing the proceeds of the sales in the colonial treasury. At the breaking out of the war Governor Hyde instructed the agents whom he sent to South Carolina to ask for military aid to represent to the colonial authorities there "the great advantage that may be made of slaves, there being many hundreds of them, women and children; may we not believe three or four thousand." The colony, indeed, found the disposal of the captives to be as profitable as had been hoped. The promised reward of slaves as pay for services rendered brought the desired Indian allies. On one occasion, Tom Blount, chief of a tribe of friendly Indians in the area of disturbance, in making arrangements with the colonial government for an attack on a certain tribe, specified that his warriors receive payment in captives, and failing these, in other commodities.

The journals of the North Carolina council for June 25, 1713, show negotiations between acting Governor Pollock and the council for the purchase of a number of Indians for shipment to the West Indies. It was sometimes a problem to provide for the captured Indians; consequently in the same year the assembly chartered a private sloop to carry away captives brought by friendly Indians.

In South Carolina, the Indian captives taken in the early war with the Kussoe were sold as slaves by governor and council with the sanction of the proprietors, who, though they had forbidden the enslavement of Indians in the temporary laws sent out to Governor Sayle in 1671, were nevertheless the first to grant the privilege of selling Indian captives from Carolina to the West Indies, as the cheapest means of encouraging the soldiers of the infant colony. Accordingly, when war broke out with the Stono Indians in 1680, Governor West, taking advantage of the precedent already established and the expressed sanction of the proprietors for such an action, offered a price for every Indian that should be taken and brought to Charleston, and obtained the funds he needed for defense by selling the Indians to the traders. The plan proved successful, so successful, in fact, as to arouse the jealousy of the proprietors, for West appropriated some of the profits for his own benefit. The proprietors sanctioned the sale of Indians taken in actual warfare for the benefit of the colony, which meant for their own benefit. Their title to the colony rested upon the claims of England to this territory by right of conquest. The Indians were the captives and the conquered people of that conquest. By the rules of war the conquered people were at the mercy and disposal of the conquerors, and since the proprietors found more profit in selling than in killing the captive Indians, they naturally resented West's taking their profits for other purposes.

By the time of the wars in the early eighteenth century, the power of the proprietors was broken, and the assembly took charge of the matter of disposing of captives in war. An act passed September 10, 1702, provided that the Indian slaves taken by the Yamasee and the other Indian allies on the expedition to St. Augustine in 1702, should be bought only by a committee of four named by the assembly. The slaves would then be disposed of to help meet the expenses of the expedition. But the committee neglected to carry out its instructions, and another act of May 8, 1703, provided that the slaves taken on the expedition might be bought by anyone, and the Indian allies be thus encouraged.

That all the Indian captives taken on the second expedition to St. Augustine in 1704 were not sold as slaves was due to an order of the assembly expressed through the governor. Moore lamented this fact, as the plunder of his men, which he estimated should have been £100 to a man, would thus be much diminished. That he still hoped with the governor's assistance "to find a way to gratify them for the loss of blood," may mean that he had not yet given up the idea of selling those Indian captives whom he called "free."

As a part of the preparation for self-defense made by South Carolina in 1707 and 1708, acts were passed giving the commanding officer of any expedition the power of commissioner to buy all prisoners of the Indian enemy above the age of twelve years that should be taken captive by the white forces or the Indian allies. The slaves so bought were to be delivered to the public receiver, who was directed to pay for them not to exceed the sum of £7 for every Indian, and then to ship them to the islands of the West Indies for sale, or to dispose of them within the colony for the use of the public to any person who would enter into bonds, with the penalty of £200, not to send or carry any slave so bought to any place within the province, or to the northward thereof. Any white person refusing to sell such slave to the commanding officer, must dispose or the slave himself, as before described, within the space of one month, or forfeit the same to the receiver for the use of the public, to be disposed of as aforesaid. In 1715, however, the law was changed so as to read that all Indian enemies captured should be handed over to the public receiver for the use of the public, the receiver to sell such as slaves to those who would pay the highest price, and who would promise to export them from the colony within the period of two months after the sale.

During the French and Indian War, the Cherokee Indians began hostilities with the English. North Carolina, in the provisions made in 1760 for raising troops against them, offered to anyone who took captive "an enemy Indian o' the right to hold him as a slave." By the treaty concluded by South Carolina with the Cherokee at the close of the war, it was provided that the captives on each side should be given up. The North Carolinians, however, followed the policy advocated in 1760, and the Indians accordingly retaliated by carrying off two white girls from South Carolina to Pensacola, and demanded, before releasing them, that those of their own people held in captivity should first be given up.

In both of the New England Indian wars discussed, the disposal of the captives fell under the immediate jurisdiction of the respective colonial governments, and was carried on either by the general court, as in the case of Massachusetts, or by a council of war which was a committee of the general court, as in the case of Plymouth. Though during the Pequot War Connecticut sent no Indians to the West Indies, still it was customary for the government to sell them out of the colony during the period following the war. This appears from a law passed in 1656 by the general court, forbidding such sale outside the boundaries of "the other three colonies," without the consent of the authorities of the plantation "under the penalty of £10 for each default."

The attitude of the New England colonial governments, so definitely expressed during the Pequot War, was continually shown from that time until King Philip's War. During that period, 1636-1675, New England was the scene of constant intertribal Indian difficulties between the Mohegan and Narraganset tribes. Because of the danger resulting from these disturbances, Massachusetts Bay, Plymouth, Connecticut and New Haven entered into confederation for mutual defense, under the name of the United Colonies of New England. The articles containing the terms of the intercolonial agreement, drawn up May 19, 1643, expressed the same spirit that was shown during the Pequot War, for they provided that "the whole advantage of the war . . . , whether it be in lands, goods or persons, shall be proportionally divided among the said confederates."

Continued disturbances led the commissioners of the United Colonies to prepare for a campaign against the Narraganset Indians in 1645. Captain John Mason was put in command of the forces raised. In keeping with the provision of the articles already mentioned, his commission, dated July, 1645, concluded thus: "what booty you take or prisoners, whether men, women or children, you may send to Seabrook fort, to be kept and improved for the advantage of the colonies in several proportions answering to their charges, etc."

During King Philip's War the various New England governments, with Massachusetts and Plymouth in the lead, again took charge of the disposal of the captive Indians. Various methods were adopted to convert their Indian captives into a source of immediate revenue. One was to sell them outright outside of the colonies, or, on occasion, within the colonies, and thus replenish the exchequer, and, so far as might be, defray the expenses of the war. At a meeting of the Plymouth Court in 1676 to consider the disposal of more than a hundred captives, the conclusion was reached, "upon serious and deliberate consideration and agitation" concerning them, "to sell the greater number into servitude." A little later, in the same year, several more were sold. In each case the colonial treasurer was ordered to effect the sale for the benefit of the colony. A fiscal report of Plymouth for the period from June 25, 1675, to September 23, 1676, gives among the credits the following, which relates to the sale of the one hundred and eighty-eight Indians already mentioned: "By the following accounts, received in, or as silver, viz.: captives, for 188 prisoners at war sold, £397 13s."

Records of similar events are found in Massachusetts Bay. On November 4, 1676, the magistrates and deputies adopted a report of a committee of the general court providing for the selling abroad of several Indians. Again, on September 16, 1676, the general court passed an act for handing over the disposal of certain captured Indians to the council. The general court expressed the opinion that such of them as had shed English blood should suffer death. The inference concerning the remainder is that they were to be sold.

A second method of paying debts by the use of captives was to direct the treasurer of the colony to dispose of a certain number of Indians, and turn the proceeds to the account of a certain individual in whose debt the colony stood; or to give a certain number of Indians to such a person, usually with the stipulation that the Indians be at once sold out of the colony. An instance of the first kind occurred in Plymouth, October 4, 1675, when the general court voted with "reference to such emergent charges that have fallen on our honored governor, the summer past, the court have settled and conferred on him, the price of ten Indians of those savages lately transported out of the government." The second method is illustrated by a later act of the Plymouth court, August 24, 1676, when, along with ten Indians ordered by the court to be delivered to Captain Benjamin Church and Captain Anthony Low for transportation out of the colony, one Indian was ordered "to be at the disposal of Henry Lilly, which he receives in full satisfaction for his attendance at this court. This Indian, like the others, was to be transported." How far the receipts from the sale of captives went toward meeting the expenses of the colony is not known. It must, however, have been but a short way, if one is to judge by the condition of the colonial exchequer at the time and the expedients adopted by the colonial government to obtain money to defend the frontiers and meet the other expenses of war.

Still a third way was to grant the captured Indians directly to those who took them prisoners, as a bounty for their capture. The Massachusetts act of 1695, which, along with the rewards for killing Indians, conferred on the soldiers for their own use all plunder and provisions taken from the enemy, appears to have been the earliest relinquishment by the provincial government of its sovereign right to prisoners and captives. In the later laws liberal premiums were continued for scalps, and volunteer captors of Indians were, by the law of 1706, granted the benefit of captives and plunder. A law of 1703 provided that the governor and council, in the absence of the general assembly, possessed the power to pay for Indian captives under ten years old the sum of £3, and stated that they could use the Indians thus obtained, either for the redemption of English captives among the Indians, or else they could sell them across the sea. Another law of the same year granted the regular forces the benefit of the sale of all Indian prisoners under the age of ten years taken by them to be transported out of the country, the profits of the sale to be shared among the officers and men of the company engaged, proportionally to their wages. All volunteers were, likewise, to have the benefit of all Indian prisoners under the age of ten years by them taken. By such legal action Massachusetts was in reality putting a premium on slave catching.

The colonial governments not only sold the Indian captives themselves, but sometimes authorized their military commanders so to do. On January 15, 1676, the governor of Massachusetts issued instructions to Captain Benjamin Church to go against the Indians, and to distribute among his men the plunder and captives according to such agreement as captain and company might make. The instructions read: "And it shall be lawful, and is hereby warranted, for him to make sale of such prisoners as their perpetual slaves; or otherwise to retain them, as they think meet (they being such as the law allows to be kept)." On August 28, 1676, also, the governor of Plymouth wrote to the governor of Rhode Island that Captain Church had been chosen and authorized by Plymouth to demand and receive of the governor of Rhode Island all the captive Indians, and to guard and conduct them to Plymouth, or to sell and dispose of them, as he chose, to the inhabitants or others for terms of life, or for shorter times, as there may be reasons.

No exception to this custom of enslavement was made in the case of the Praying Indians. During the course of the war several of these Indians, "through the harsh dealings of the English" and because of neglect to provide them with "sufficient shelter, protection and encouragement," joined the warring Indians. Such of these Indians as were taken in arms were declared by the Massachusetts general court to be in rebellion, and were tried and sentenced, some to be killed, but the most of them to be transported and sold as slaves.

Captives were also retained as slaves in the colony, especially the women and children. For instance, in 1675, in return for the privilege granted by Mr. Shrimpton of Noddle's Island to quarter one hundred Indians upon that island free of charge, the general court of Massachusetts ordered five Christian Indian prisoners to be delivered to him to be employed on Noddle's Island, "he returning them to the order of the council."

It is very probable, as Gookin asserts, that instances are not lacking in which some of the Praying Indians were sold as slaves under accusations which were false. Such happened also in the case of other Indians. Their promises were not considered sincere by the colonial authorities, for a result of the war was an intense hatred and suspicion of all Indians. The Praying Indians were sufficiently numerous to be a dangerous factor, and the colonial authorities intended to give them no chance to gain the advantage.

Whatever may have been the number of enslaved Indian captives retained in Massachusetts, that number was sufficiently large to cause some uneasiness on the part of both authorities and people. On July 22, 1676, the general court of Plymouth confirmed an act of the council of war declaring that, because of the danger to the peace and safety of the colony incurred by having Indian captives residing there, no male captive above the age of fourteen years of age should reside in the colony; and that, if any such captive above that age was then resident in the colony, he was to be disposed of out of the colony before October 15, 1676, or be forfeited to the government. It is not likely that the act was rigorously enforced during its brief existence. Exceptions to the law were doubtless made by the court from time to time.

Another act of similar tenor was passed March 29, 1677, when the Massachusetts council in an order, the preamble of which shows much alarm on the part of the people, decreed that no one within the colony should thereafter buy or keep, more than ten days after the publication of the Council's decree, any Indian men or women already bought, above the age of twelve years, without allowance from authority. A fine of £5, and the forfeit of the Indian or Indians concerned were fixed as a penalty for violation of the law. Toward the end of the year Plymouth still further extended governmental supervision of captives by decreeing, March 5, 1678, that no one was to buy the children of the captive Indians taken during the late war, "without special leave, liking and approbation of the government of this jurisdiction."

The seizure of Indians by authority of the colonial governments, and their subsequent sale, were not always above suspicion. At the time of the Narraganset troubles, in 1646, Plymouth gave legal sanction for the seizure of peaceable and unsuspecting Indians whose tribes were at peace with the English. A second instance of the same character occurred during King Philip's War shortly after the destruction of Dartmouth in 1675. The Dartmouth Indians had not been concerned in the burning of the town, so the whites entered into negotiations of peace and friendship with them, and the captains of the resident militia and the Plymouth forces sent thither promised them protection. But through other influences they were conducted to Plymouth, and, by order of the council, August 4, 1675, they were sold and transported out of the Country, being about Eight-score Persons. On September 2, 1675, the council took similar action in the case of "a parcel of Indians lately come into Sandwich, in a submissive way to this colony." They were adjudged to be "in the same condition of rebellion," and were condemned, fifty-seven in number, to perpetual servitude.

A fourth, and far more notable instance of bad faith on the part of the English, occurred at Cocheco (Dover, New Hampshire) during the Indian difficulties in that section, contemporaneous with and following King Philip's War. Major Waldron was in command of the local garrison, and had gathered about him four hundred Indians, about two hundred of whom were refugees who had fled there for protection after the death of King Philip, which Waldron had promised them. The depredations of the Androscoggin Indians at Casco and the devastation of the settlements on the Kennebec caused the Massachusetts government to send a military force into that locality, with orders to seize all southern Indians wherever they could find them. In obedience to this order the leaders of the Massachusetts troops wished to seize the Indians at once, but Waldron hesitated to break his promise and proposed a stratagem to avoid disastrous results. His suggestion was followed, and all the Indians were disarmed and made prisoners, September 7, 1676. The "strange Indians," or those who had come from the south, two hundred in number, were retained and sent to Boston. Seven or eight who were convicted of having shed English blood were condemned to death; the rest were sold into slavery in foreign parts.

Toward the close of the war orders were given by certain of the New England colonies to the constables to seize all Indians remaining in the colonies after a specific date. All who had been concerned in the death of a colonist or the destruction of property were to be summarily executed. Those who remained friendly or had finally assisted the English, were allowed to retain their lands and continue their regular life. The others were to be sold by the treasurers of the various colonies for the benefit of their respective governments.

The locating of those Indians that remained after the war, and the necessity of maintaining order, resulted, 1677, in the government of Massachusetts settling the groups of Indians, Praying as well as unconverted, in various localities, and the distribution of some to "remain as servants in English families" where they were to be taught and instructed in the Christian religion. Both the captive male Indians and their families were held as slaves. Massachusetts and Plymouth limited the time of servitude of the children of "friendly Indians," or those who surrendered and assisted the English, to the time when they should become twenty-four years of age. The time of service of the children of the warring Indians was not so limited.

Since King Philip's War was never carried into Connecticut territory, the problem of disposing of Indian captives never assumed the same importance there as in Massachusetts, and the Connecticut government did not export its captive Indians. On October 23, 1676, as a measure intended to induce the surrender of the warring tribes and so hasten the conclusion of the war, the general court ordered that all Indians who surrendered before January 1, 1677, should not be sold out of the country as slaves. The measure, however, permitted their use as temporary slaves in the colony. They were to receive good usage in the service of those to whom the council might dispose of them, and after ten years, all over sixteen years of age, on certificate of good behavior from their masters regarding their good service during that period, were to have their liberty and be allowed to dwell in the colony and work for themselves, provided they observed English law. If the master should refuse such certificate, then the Indian could apply to the authorities and have his case decided. The council was given power to lengthen the term of servitude if it should see cause, but could not shorten it. All Indians under sixteen years of age were to serve until twentysix years of age.

At a meeting, November 24, 1676, the Connecticut council decided upon its method of procedure. A committee was appointed to meet at Norwich on the second Wednesday of the following

December to "dispose and settle all surrenders according to order." All Indians expecting to have the benefit of the declaration must then and there appear. After that time all those who had shown hostility to the English were excluded from the privilege and were to be dealt with as enemies, as were also those who should hide or harbor them. The notice of the council's action was to be sent among the various Indians of the colony. The instructions of the committee appointed directed them, among other things, to take all young and single persons of all sorts to put into English families to be apprentices for ten years. After that they were to be returned to their parents on proof of their own and their parents' fidelity. Otherwise they were to be sold into slavery. The general court appointed certain persons in each county to receive and distribute these Indian children proportionally, and to see that they were sold to good families. Those counties which had already had some share of the surrendered Indians and captives or which had too many Indians already, were not to receive as many as the other counties.

The Rhode Island authorities also limited the bondage of Indians to a period of years. On May 18, 1652, the colony passed a law that no black mankind or white should be forced by covenant, bond or otherwise, to serve any man or his assignees longer than ten years, or until they became twenty-four years of age, if they be taken in under fourteen, from the time of their coming within the limits of the colony; and at the end of the term of ten years, they were to be set free, "as the manner is with English servants."

Either the framers of the law intended that Indians be included under the terms "black mankind or white," or else the subject of Indian slavery had not yet attracted the attention of the law makers at this time. Probably the latter is the true explanation of the omission of the term "Indian" from the act, though at a later time the same restriction of service was applied to Indians without legislation.

On March 13, 1676, the general assembly convened at Newport and discussed the Indian situation. An order was given that "no Indian in this colony shall be a slave," save only for debts, covenant, etc., "as if they had been Countrymen not at war." But Rhode Island did not avail itself of every opportunity to retain captive Indians. On one occasion the assembly voted, June 30, 1676, to send back to Plymouth a number of Indians whom Roger Williams had sent there, because they believed the Indians rightly belonged to the northern colony. Again, on August 23, 1676, the government held a court martial for the trial of some Indians whom the Rhode Island troops had Captured. Several of these Indians were sentenced to death for crimes against the English. Others were freed. None was retained in the colony.

The assembly made an earnest effort to prevent the indiscriminate and unfair sale of Indians not taking part in the war, by forbidding during its session in August, 1676, that any Indians be brought into the colony without permission of the governor and two assistants, under penalty of a fine of £5 and the forfeit of such Indian or Indians. The sum of the fine and the forfeited Indians were "to return to the treasurer of each town." All persons were declared to be entitled to half the produce of the Indians whom they might legally bring to Newport. The other half was to go to the treasury. If such an amount was not paid in, the said Indians were to be forfeited to the treasurer of the colony. It was also forbidden to carry any Indian away from the colony without a permit from the governor, deputy-governor or two magistrates, upon penalty of the forfeiture of £5. All acts, orders, commissions, verbal orders, etc., which had been issued by town councils, councils of war, private orders of officers and "other ministers of justice," which related to Indians, were declared legal by the assembly.

Such action as that referred to in this measure was taken at a town meeting in Portsmouth, March 8, 1675. The meeting, fearing that the holding of Indian slaves might prove "prejudicial" ordered that all persons of the town having any Indian slave of either sex should be given but one month to sell and send such out of the town, and that no inhabitant after that time should buy or keep an Indian slave under penalty of £5 fine for each month thus holding such a slave, the amount of the fine to be paid to the town treasurer.

It was politic for the colonial governments to oppose the enslavement of Indians who were friendly to the English or in alliance with them. Two such instances are recorded in connection with North Carolina. In 1713, at the request of the governor of New York, the Seneca Indians sent an Indian to the Tuscarora to caution them against going to war with the English. The South Carolina Indians captured this Indian and held him as a slave. The council decided to buy him and send him back to his own nation. In the same year the council ordered that a colonist who had sold a friendly Indian as a slave should be held for trial.

During the intercolonial wars the French Indians were accustomed to take both their white and red captives to Canada, where the latter became slaves. As a part of their protective, diplomatic and military policy, the English sought to regain the freedom of these Indians, and thus retain the friendship of the Six Nations. In 1688, Governor Dongan demanded of the French agents that certain New York Indians who had been sent from Canada to France, be returned to the English consul at Paris or to the authorities in London, so that they might be brought home and be given their freedom. The French authorities agreed, and the Indians were brought back. In 1748, Governor Shirley sought to obtain the freedom of a Rhode Island Indian who had been sold as a slave in Canada, and on another occasion sent fourteen French prisoners to South Carolina to redeem certain members of the Six Nations who were held there. Throughout the French and Indian struggle the governors of New York insisted that the members of the Six Nations, when captured in war, should be treated exactly as other English subjects, or, in other words, that they should not be enslaved.

CHAPTER VI. PROCESSES OF ENSLAVEMENT: KIDNAPPING

THE process of obtaining Indians by kidnapping was common to the early English explorers in America, as well as to those of Spain and France. In 1498, the expedition of Sebastian Cabot brought back to England three natives from the New World. Lord Bacon states that two of the Indians "were seen two years afterward, dressed like Englishmen, and not to be distinguished from them." The Cabots had set off, promising to bring home heavy cargoes of spices and oriental gems. They returned with empty ships and with nothing to relate concerning the sought-for land of Cathay. Their expedition had not reached its desired destination, but some of the natives would serve as proof of another land discovered, and would, perhaps, provoke sufficient interest to assure the fitting out of a second expedition. These Indians were not destined for the slave markets, and were probably kept as curiosities.

England still hoped to find the northwest passage to the Orient. In 1576, Frobisher made another attempt in that direction. He desired to take away some token as proof of his having been in the New World, and, as it was supposed the Indians had destroyed or stolen three of his men who were lost, he decided to take some savages captive by luring them to trade. In this way one was captured, but died on reaching England. A similar instance occurred on the second voyage in 1577. Frobisher planned to seize several Indians, bestow gifts upon them, and send them to their own people, hoping thus to win the friendship of the natives, after keeping one of them as interpreter. An attempt was made to seize two, but one escaped. As a companion for this man, an Indian woman was afterward captured. Frobisher attempted to trade these captives for Some lost Englishmen, but was unsuccessful; so it is probable that they were carried to England. The relation of the third voyage, 1578, mentions a similar man and woman, but the narrator does not state whether these were the same two taken on the second voyage, carried to England, and brought back to America on the third voyage, or two others taken on the third voyage. These Indians provoked much curiosity and comment in England, and pictures of them were made for the queen and others.

The search for the northwest passage was continued by Captain George Weymouth in 1605, under the patronage of Lord Popham and Sir Ferdinando Gorges. Weymouth reached the coast of America at the mouth of the present Penobscot River in Maine. By making presents to the Indians and by treating them kindly, he induced five of them to come on board his ship. These five Indians were kidnapped and carried to England, along with their canoes and the personal belongings which they had with them at the time of capture. There appears to have been no feeling of opposition shown to such an act. Three of them were presented by Weymouth to Gorges, and two to Popham. Gorges declared that "this accident must be acknowledged the means under God of putting on foot and giving life to all our plantations." Weymouth did not propose to obtain financial profit by the sale of these Indians any more than did his predecessors, Cabot and Frobisher. His immediate purpose was probably to please his patrons by a curious gift, and doubtless he shared the purpose of Gorges and Popham of learning from them the resources of their native land, and by instructing them, to have them fitted to act as intelligent guides and interpreters in some future expedition. His instructions required that he treat the Indians kindly so that they might prove friendly to future settlements. The treatment of the captives in England was evidently kind. Gorges kept his Indians in his family three years and obtained from them the knowledge he desired. The Indians were shown to the curious, perhaps for money, and it has been held that one, after death, was exhibited for an admission price.

Captain Edward Harlow, under the patronage of the Earl of Southampton, visited America in 1611, and at "Monhigan Island" seized three Indians who had come on board to trade. One of these escaped and incited his friends to revenge, so Harlow proceeded southward and from the islands in the vicinity of Cape Cod kidnapped three others. With these five Indians he returned to England.

Though in the cases cited the Indians taken by the English were probably not destined to actual slavery, yet instances are not wanting in which they were taken for that purpose. The profit to be derived from the sales in the slave markets was tempting. Just before sending out the expedition of 1614, Captain Henry Harley brought to Gorges a native of the island of Capawick (Martha's Vineyard.) This Indian had been captured with some twenty-nine others by a ship from London and taken to Spain for sale as a slave. The sale failed wholly or in part, and some of the Indians were brought to England and shown as curiosities as the other Indians had been. Gorges, though he had sanctioned the act of Weymouth, condemned the action of the captors of this group of Indians, for he feared the Indians of America would be unfriendly to colonial enterprise.

The London ship above mentioned was one commanded by Thomas Hunt, and formed part of Smith's expedition for the carrying of fish, furs and oil from New England to Virginia and Malaga. Smith took the first ship to Virginia and left Hunt to take the other to Spain with a cargo of dry fish. But a cargo of slaves seemed to offer greater gain than one of fish. Twenty-seven Indians were taken captive off the Massachusetts coast and sent to Spain. Among this number was Tisquantum (called Squantum by the English), who had formerly been captured by Weymouth, and who had been returned to America. Some of the Indians were sold in Spain for £20 apiece. By the interference of some monks the further sale of the Indians was prevented, and Squantum, at least, was carried off to England. When Gorges sent out Captain Hobson to America two of Hunt's captives accompanied him, but, on arrival, they escaped and so aroused their friends that a settlement by Hobson was prevented. This feeling of suspicion and hatred toward the English must have found expression, if it had not been prevented by the deadly pestilence of 1616 which weakened the Indians of New England, and by the intercession of Squantum who proved a firm friend of the English in arranging a treaty with the Indians. Hunt's act was done entirely on his own responsibility and without the knowledge or sanction of Smith who denounced it as a vile deed, since it ever afterward kept him from trading in those parts.

The evidence of kidnapping in the southern colonies seems very meagre. The existing records deal chiefly with other modes of obtaining Indians for slaves. There were undoubtedly many cases of kidnapping pure and simple, if we may judge by the general attitude of the colonists toward the Indians; but kidnapping, considered as distinct from any sort of warfare, was not a suitable means of producing the number of Indians needed or desired by the Carolina colonists. Trade and war were more prolific means, and hence were more largely used. Kidnapping was a process of obtaining slaves suited only to a locality, or to an occasion when but few Indians were desired.

Yet certain incidents show the custom was practiced here as elsewhere. An event of 1685 is probably only one of many such which occurred on the southern coast and in the interior at the time of the Indian disturbances in that Section, before war had actually begun. In that year a vessel from New York kidnapped four Indians in the locality of Cape Fear, North Carolina, and carried them to New York for sale. That there was a certain amount of kidnapping carried on in the other southern colonies, as Virginia and Maryland, is shown by the colonial legislation regarding the matter, which will be discussed later.

It has been seen that it was customary to enslave Indian captives taken in war, and that certain colonial governments even allowed the seizure of peaceable Indians in time of war, lest they join with the warring Indians. The distinction between kidnapping, pure and simple, and seizures made in time of war, was too delicate to be always observed, and was open to abuse by unscrupulous persons desiring to obtain Indians for sale. Nowhere is this more clearly exemplified than in the New England colonies. Here, as in the south, kidnapping was carried on by the frontier people who were generally rough and lawless. Along with indifference to the rights of the Indians, fraudulent practices in trade, and refusal to sell them arms and ammunition on the slightest suspicion that the weapons might be used against the whites, the kidnapping of Indians, and the selling of them as slaves in the West Indies were all numbered among the causes of King Philip's War.

With the opening of King Philip's War the custom was continued. The Maine Indians were about to join those in Massachusetts when, through the efforts of Abraham Shurt of Pemaquid, and by means of promises made to right their wrongs and treat the native fairly in the future, the union with the Massachusetts Indians was prevented, and assurances of friendship were exchanged with the English. Rumors were soon spread abroad, however, that the Indians were possessed of arms, and were forming a conspiracy against the colony. The government became alarmed and issued a warrant to General Waldron of Cocheco (Dover, New Hampshire) "to seize every Indian known to be a man slayer, traitor or conspirator." Waldron took it upon himself to issue general warrants for this purpose. These warrants fell into the hands of unprincipled men who set about using them to immediate advantage. A vessel was fitted out at Pemaquid and a crew organized for the purpose of kidnapping Indians for sale abroad. Shurt remonstrated with the leaders of the proceeding and warned the Indians of their danger. But the plan succeeded, at least in part. A vessel off Pemaquid, commanded by one Laughton, succeeded during the winter of 1676 in capturing several Indians, and carrying them abroad for sale. The Indians complained of this action, but the only satisfaction they obtained was more offers of friendship and the promise that means should be taken to return their captured friends to them. Waldron was indicted by the grand jury for surprising and stealing seventeen Indians, carrying them off to Fayal in the vessel *Endeavor* and selling them there, but was acquitted. John Laughton, captain of the vessel, was also indicted for the same offenses, found guilty by the Court of General Sessions, and fined £20. More pressing matters engaged the attention of the authorities for some time, and no further attention was given to this event.

Not even Pennsylvania was free from the custom. In 1710, the Indians manifested some uneasiness, and when the governor sent a committee to learn their wishes they returned eight wanpum belts which represented their requests. One belt signified, so the Indians explained to the committee, that their old women desired the friendship of the Christians and Indians of the government, and the privilege to fetch wood and water without danger and trouble; another, that their children might have room to play and sport without danger of slavery. The young men begged that they might be granted the privilege to hunt without fear of death or slavery; and the chiefs desired a lasting peace that thereby they might be secured against those "fearful apprehensions they had felt for several years." A similar complaint was made by the "Senoquois" to Lieutenant-Governor Gookin. The Indians asserted that one Francis La Tore had taken a boy from them and had sold him in New York, and requested the lieutenant-governor to inquire about him.

Whether or not actual kidnapping of the natives occurred in New York, at least the Indians were familiar with the custom as practiced by the whites. The following is a case in point. When the Moravian missionaries first visited New York, early in the eighteenth century, the whites, in order to counteract the influence of Rauch, one of these missionaries who was working at the Indian town of Shekomeka east of the Hudson River, told the Indians of that section that the missionary intended to seize their young people, carry them beyond the seas and sell them into slavery.

Events in New York illustrate another phase of Indian kidnapping. During the war between Spain and the United Netherlands prizes were occasionally brought by privateers to New Amsterdam from the Caribbean islands and the Spanish Main. Part of the cargoes of these vessels consisted of kidnapped Spanish Indians. Their presence in the colony was considered undesirable and their seizure generally unfair, for they were in some cases of Spanish as well as Indian blood. After peace was declared between Spain and the Netherlands, 1648, hostilities still continued between Spain and France. To privateers flying the French flag, New Amsterdam was a neutral port where captive negroes and other prize goods were sold. Among these negroes was Sometimes found a Spanish Indian. In 1692, and again in 1699, laws were passed to suppress privateering. But, despite these laws, the practice was adhered to, and the number of free Spanish Indians held in New York increased. A petition to the governor of New York, in 1711, shows a free Indian woman, a resident of Southampton, kidnapped and sold as a slave in Madeira, from whence she was returned by the English consul to New York. This instance illustrates the work of pirates also.

Mention is frequently found of Spanish Indians in other colonies, especially in New England. Cotton Mather records buying a Spanish Indian and giving him to his father. Mayhew mentions the death of Chilmark, a Spanish Indian brought from some part of the Spanish Indies when he was a boy and sold in New England. The New England and other newspapers contain frequent mention of Spanish Indian runaways and Spanish Indians for sale in Massachusetts,

Connecticut, Rhode Island and Pennsylvania. The *Boston News Letter* of July 31, 1704, and October 28, 1706, mentions both negro and Indian slaves taken off the coast of New Spain by privateers fitted out in South Carolina. It may be that the so-called Spanish mulatto kidnapped by a privateer, sold in the colony of Pennsylvania and freed by the council in 1703, was a Spanish Indian.

Considering the prevalence of piracy and privateering during the colonial period, it seems probable that there were not a few Spanish Indians brought to the different colonies in this way and in the cargoes of negroes from the West Indies and Brazil, whose existence in the colonies was never brought to the attention of the colonial authorities.

Kidnapping of Indians was contrary to express statute in most, if not in all the colonies, and to the law of nations as generally recognized in the international intercourse of Europeans with heathen and barbarian nations. There was considerable legislative action in the different colonies intended to check the practice, which had, however, but little effect. In some of the colonies laws were passed intending to put an end to the practice by providing fines and penalties for the kidnapping of Indians. In other colonies legislative or executive action dealt, not with the custom in general, but with certain specific events which aroused attention or were brought by someone concerned directly to the notice of the legislative body or the executive. One thing is apparent throughout all the legislation on this subject: the absence of any particular sympathy for of the Indian himself. In some cases the Indian was only included incidentally or by implication in a general law which made no specific mention of him. In other cases laws against kidnapping were passed because of the effect that kidnapping might have on the Indians within or surrounding the colony. In short, the motive was the desire for selfprotection dictated by fear of disastrous results, rather than by any humanitarian feeling.

It has been seen that kidnapping concerned two classes of Indians, those taken in English territory, and those taken in Spanish territory and brought to the English colonies.

Colonial legislation and executive action included both classes.

The Virginia act of 1657 aimed directly at the stealing of Indian children by Indians who had been hired by the English. All such stolen children were to be returned to their own tribe within ten days, and five hundred pounds of tobacco were to be paid by the offending party to the informer of such kidnapping.

In 1672, the council of Maryland forbade the carrying of a certain friendly Indian out of the colony without special license from the governor. In 1692, for the sake of preserving peace with the neighboring Indians, a law was enacted forbidding any one to "entice, surprise, transport, or cause to be transported, or sell or dispose of any friendly Indian or Indians whatsoever, or endeavor or attempt so to do, without license from the governor for the time being, and offering a reward to any informer of such an event." The same law was reënacted in 1705.

Article ninety-one of the Massachusetts Body of Liberties of 1641 provided that no one except captives taken in just wars etc. should be held as slaves in the colony. In 1649, the Body of Liberties was reënforced by a law decreeing: "If any man stealeth a man or mankind, he shall surely be put to death." Some attention was given to enforcing this law, for the records show an occasional imprisonment for stealing Indians. On July 4, 1667, the governor of Barbadoes sent back to Massachusetts two Indians that had been taken to England and then carried to Barbadoes and sold as slaves. In an accompanying address to the governor and assistants of Massachusetts he promised to rectify all such abuses that might come under his jurisdiction. But in spite of laws and precautions the practice of kidnapping continued throughout the colonial period.

Other colonies followed the example of Massachusetts in making man-stealing a capital crime. New Jersey, in 1675, and New Hampshire, in 1679, enacted similar laws. Just how far the laws were intended to relate to kidnapped Indians is a matter for conjecture. They were in all probability intended to apply to the stealing of negro slaves, and there is nothing in their content to show that they were intended to relate also to the stealing of free Indians.

CHAPTER VII. PROCESSES OF ENSLAVEMENT: TRADE

IN all sections where captives in war or kidnapped Indians were purchased from the natives, such buying was closely connected with the fur trade. The general fickleness and instability of the Indian's character, which caused the tribes to change their allegiance so readily from one white race to the other, made easy the acquisition of slaves along with other commodities. The routes along which the fur trade was carried on facilitated both the acquisition of Indians and their transportation to the markets. And the fact that furs and the agricultural products of the south were not commodities that competed with English wares eliminated opposition to the traffic in Indians.

Throughout the region of the Mississippi Valley and the Great Lakes the "coureurs de bois" collected furs and purchased slaves, both of which they sold to Carolina traders at the mouth of the Mississippi River, and in some cases they went to the Carolinas directly to effect their sales. Throughout the Carolinas, the Mississippi and Illinois country and the west, the fur and Indian trade was heavy. By 1720 the Carolina fur trade had reached very large dimensions, and the trade in Indians had developed proportionally, so that at "set times of the year" a flourishing business in "dressed deer skins, furs and young Indian slaves" was carried on by the traders.

In the Carolinas the custom of purchasing their prisoners from the friendly Indians, the holding of these captives in the colony as slaves, or, possibly, their subsequent sale to the West India islands, existed almost from the beginning of the colony. But the proprietors, anxious to cultivate the friendship of the Indians, forbade, in the temporary laws sent out to Governor Sayle in 1671, that any Indian on any pretext whatever be made a slave, or without his own consent be carried out of the country.

Yet the traffic in Indians continued. The adventurous nature of the settlers, combined with the need for laborers which could be partially supplied by the use of Indians at home or by the negroes for whom they could be readily exchanged in the islands, and coupled with the attraction of good prices which the Indians brought when sold for cash, induced both planters and government officials to enter largely into the trade.

To supply the ever-increasing demand for Indian slaves, the tribes of the south and southwest constantly preyed upon each other. The matter of international rivalry also entered largely into the policy of the Carolinians. The Indians of the south and west were divided in their allegiance to the three white races, Spanish, French and English. Each of these three nations sought not only to win and hold the allegiance of as many of the tribes as possible, but also to use these tribes to strike at its rival's allies, and the readiness with which the English, especially, bought the captives for slaves served to keep up a continuous series of depredations of tribe upon tribe.

The Westo, an important tribe on the southern border of South Carolina, furnished a number of such captives during the latter part of the eighteenth century in spite of their two treaties made with the proprietors, 1677 and 1678, in which they promised not to prey upon the smaller and weaker tribes who were friends and allies of the English. In 1693, the Cherokee sent a delegation to Governor Smith of South Carolina to complain of the Esaw, Congaree, and Savannah who were preying upon those tribes and selling the captives thus obtained as slaves to the English. The Savannah, like the Westo, were so acting in violation of their treaty by which they agreed not to molest neighboring tribes. In 1706, English Indian allies attacked Pensa and carried off members of the Apalachee tribe for so as slaves. On July 10, 1708, Thomas Maine, an agent of the general assembly of South Carolina, reported to that body that the Talapoosa and the Chickasaw, incited by the good prices which the traders offered them for captives, were engaged in making slaves of the Indians on the lower Mississippi who were subject to the French. In this instance one finds the usual excuse given by the English in such cases: " some men think it both serves to lessen their number before the French can arm them, and it is a more effective way of civilizing and instructing them than all the efforts used by the French missionaries".

The French asserted that the policy of the English of Carolina in setting one Indian tribe against another was a part of their plan for driving the French from Louisiana and the Mississippi River country. The process of obtaining Indian slaves through trade was, then, a part of a great political contest. The alliance of the leading tribes, such as the Chickasaw and the Choctaw, meant much to both English and

French from the territorial and the commercial standpoints. In consequence, no effort was spared by either of the white races to obtain a dominating influence over these tribes in order to use them for their own benefit. This benefit consisted largely of the gain in trade both in furs and slaves. The French sought to dissolve this friendship by telling the Chickasaw that the English were only seeking destroy them by having them wage war for slaves, and that when they were sufficiently weakened by war the English would fall upon them and sell them all as slaves.

In consequence of the unstable nature of the Indian and the influence brought to bear upon the tribes by both French and English, it was but natural that Indian relations in the section east of the lower Mississippi should be kaleidoscopic in character. As each tribe gave, or refused to give, allegiance to the English it was in turn preyed upon by the English allies. If one is to accept the assertions of the French in the early eighteenth century, the Chickasaw during their eight or ten years intercourse with the English lost five hundred prisoners, and the Choctaw, eight hundred, sold as slaves by the English.

The opening of the War of the Spanish Succession increased the activity of both English and French among the Indians and the consequent preying of tribe upon tribe. The French asserted that they established their colony at Mobile for the purpose of keeping the savages of the neighborhood as allies of the French and Spanish against the English and Chickasaw whose purpose, in their opinion, was to win them over or else destroy them by enslavement. By 1700 the English of Carolina had crossed the Mississippi River and on the west bank pursued the same tactics with the Indians as elsewhere. Slaves were obtained by the English and Chickasaw from nations as far distant as the Taensa. In furtherance of their scheme to win the friendship of the warlike Chickasaw, and so strike a blow at the English and protect their allies from the slave raids of the former, the French repeatedly sought to make peace between the Chickasaw and Choctaw. But the English influence was too strong for such a peace to be permanent so long as the Choctaw remained allies of the English. The peace arranged by Bienville in 1703 was broken in 1705 by the Chickasaw making an irruption into the territory of the Choctaw, capturing a number of their people and selling them to the

English of Carolina. A later peace arranged by Bienville was no more permanent, for in 1711 the Chickasaw, at the instigation of the English, fell upon the Choctaw and word was brought to Bienville that three hundred Choctaw women and children had been carried off as slaves by the Indian allies of the English and Chickasaw, and that the Chickasaw themselves had carried off one hundred and fifty. By 1713 English traders and agents were among the Natchez Indians to purchase Indians whom the French accused them of obtaining by exciting the tribes against each other.

In their relations with the Indians the Carolina proprietors appear to have been playing a double game. They posed as protectors of the tribes and made treaties to insure the peace and safety of their allies. Consistently with such action, also, they opposed the purchase by the colonists of captives taken in various intertribal difficulties. On the other hand, it was the proprietors themselves who gave permission to sell in the West Indies the Indian captives taken by the colonists in wars against the tribes. The distinction, if any existed, between the classes of captives obtained in various ways and held as slaves, was too fine a one for the colonists to appreciate; hence the purchase and sale of Indians continued.

In short, the whole attitude of the proprietors on the subject came primarily from jealousy for the colonial officials, and not from feelings of humanity or sympathy with the Indians. They opposed any action of the colonial officials which tended to make them independent of the proprietors' authority. This explains why they removed the deputies, Mathews, Moore and Middleton, and Governor West, also, in 1683, for selling Indians to the West Indies. News, in fact, had reached the proprietors that the dealers in Indians were the "greatest sticklers" against having the parliament elected according to the proprietors' instructions, so drastic measures were necessary. The fact that the proprietors chose to succeed West, Sir John Yeamans, a man filled with the slave sentiment of Barbadoes, is sufficient evidence that they entertained no hostile feelings against the system of slavery in general.

A secondary reason for the opposition of the Carolina proprietors to Indian slavery lay in the fact that the stirring up of the tribes by the colonists in order to obtain captives for slaves resulted in danger and damage to the colony, which necessarily meant financial loss to the proprietors. To carry out the idea of protecting the Indians, the grand council, in accordance with previous instructions from its superiors, sent two agents to visit the plantations in 1680 and bring to Charleston all Indian slaves whom the Westo had sold to the planters. These slaves were set at liberty. In the same year, the proprietors appointed a commission to prevent the trade in Indians and to decide all cases arising in future between Indians and English. The commission proved a failure and was abolished in 1682 on the ground that it was used for the oppression instead of the protection of the natives.

The proprietors continued their directions to the governors regarding the sale of Indians. On May 10, 1682, they instructed Governor Joseph Moreton that upon no pretense or reason whatsoever was he to suffer any Indian to be sent away from Carolina, asserting that they had taken into their protection as subjects of England all the Indians within four hundred miles of Charleston. Hence the Indians must not be made slaves in war, or in any way injured by the colonists without proprietary permission. Additional instructions, September 30, 1683, forbade the governor and council to allow the transportation of any Indians without the consent of the parliament, and gave the palatine's court, to be assembled by the governor and council for the purpose, the privilege of proposing such an act to the parliament. Any officer commissioned by the council or chosen by the palatine's court who transported Indians without a license was to be at once dismissed.

A battle royal was now on between the proprietors, with perhaps a small number of sympathizers in the parliament, on the one hand, and the council and traders on the other. The proprietors made inquiries regarding the selling of Indians both from the council and from private individuals. In a letter, September 30, 1686, also, they set forth their dissatisfaction with the condition of affairs and asserted their belief that "the private gains made by some by buying slaves of the Indians had more to do with the opinion that they ought to be transported than any consideration of public safety or benefit."

The dealers in Indians stated three reasons for the traffic: that the Savannah, having united all their tribes, had become so powerful that it was dangerous to disoblige them; that South Carolina was at war with the Waniah in which the Savannah assisted; that humanity decreed the buying of their slaves to keep them from "a cruel death." These reasons for the traffic were held by the proprietors to be unsound. They declared the buying of slaves from the Savannah alone, and the forbidding of such buying from the other Indians would serve not only to keep the Savannah united, but would join the other tribes to them and so strengthen them that they would be a danger to the colony. The war with the Waniah, they thought, had been the result of a quarrel that the whites picked for the purpose of obtaining Indians to transport. If the Savannah were to take captive the Waniah and sell them to the dealers in Indians, it was only to those few dealers who had a share in the government. These dealers had resorted to subterfuge in order to force the Savannah to sell only to them. The emissaries of peace sent by the Westo and the Waniah to the Savannah, declared the proprietors, had been seized by the last named and sold to the dealers, thus prolonging both the Waniah and the Westo wars, and likely to cause other wars. By purchasing slaves from the Savannah, also, these Indians were encouraged to make raids upon their weaker neighbors. Such activities when discussed in England prevented settlers from going to South Carolina, fearing lest the runaway negroes could not be brought back on so large a continent unless the Indians were preserved. Finally, said the proprietors, God's blessing could not be expected on a government so managed.

The proprietors, however, did not wish to forbid the selling of Indians. They recognized the usefulness, as West had done, of permitting "soldiers for their encouragement, to make the best advantage that they can out of their prisoners"; but they wanted the initiative in the matter to rest with themselves. Accordingly they authorized the parliament to pass acts for the exportation of "such Indians as they should decide upon," the said Indians to be shown in the house and examined by sworn interpreters as to their capture, name and station. The license issued by the parliament was to specify the person to whom the leave of exportation was granted. The decision of the parliament was to be rendered by a majority of the house. This license was not granted by a standing order, but for "each batch." Anyone exporting Indians without such a license was to receive the utmost punishment prescribed by law.

During his administration, John Archdale, consistent with his religious persuasion of Quaker and his political position of proprietor, did what he could to check the traffic in Indians. In 1695, a party of Yamasee (English Indians) fell upon a party of Spanish Indians not far from St. Augustine, took them prisoners and brought them to Charleston for sale to the English islands as slaves. On examining the captives and finding that they were Christians, Archdale ordered the chief of the Yamasee to return them to the Spanish governor. The difficulty of restraining Indian tribes from revenging themselves upon their enemies and selling their captives as slaves, Archdale himself records.

In 1700, James Moore forced the council to annul the election of Moreton as governor, and was himself chosen for the office. He then packed council and assembly with his associates and followers. These persons at once proceeded to use their offices for their own financial benefit, and one of the means practiced to that end was the selling of Indians to the islands of the West Indies. Moore issued commissions to persons to capture all the Indians they could for his own profit. At his instigation the Apalachee attacked the missions of Santa Catalina, on the island of that name off the coast of the present state of Georgia, and the mission of Santa Fé in Florida, burned the villages, massacred many Christian Indians and carried off others to be sold as slaves in Carolina. The members of the assembly and other inhabitants of the colony, June 26, 1705, complained to the proprietors of Moore's enslaving Indians, not on the grounds of justice and humanity, but of expediency. His action was ruining the Indian trade by creating confusion among the Indians, and would, they feared, arouse an Indian war. The proprietors denounced the governor but did not stop the practice.

By 1707 the activities of the traders in Indian slaves had become so notorious that the South Carolina assembly took up the consideration of means to remedy the matter. A board of commissioners, nine in number, was appointed to have entire charge of the subject. By them it was declared that one condition of a trader's license and bond should provide against the seizure of free Indians. Provision was also made for the appointment of Indian agents with residence (except a vacation of two months) among the Indians, said agents to give a bond of £200 and receive a yearly salary of £250. Their term of office was limited to one year. But conditions became worse after the appointment of the board than before. Indian slaves were constantly brought to Charleston and sold openly in the market place. Unprincipled men were granted trading privileges and made Indian agents. A report on the condition of the colony in 1708 shows that these slaves were sold in Boston, Rhode Island, Pennsylvania, New Jersey, Virginia and the West Indies.

It was the purpose of the assembly to have the board regulate the trade and keep it in the hands of the government. Its agents were required to take the following oath: "I, A. B., do promise and declare that I will well and truly observe and perform all the powers, orders and instructions, as shall be from time to time given or sent to me by the present commissioners, and that I will not embezzle or make away with any goods, wares, merchandise, skins, furs, slaves, or other good or liquors whatsoever, that shall be entrusted or given in charge to me or come into my hands, belonging to the public, and that I will not directly or indirectly trade with any Indian whatsoever for any skins, furs or slaves, but for the sole use of the public; and that I will keep secret and not divulge the debates and resolutions of this Board, so help me God."

Further directions required that the agents buy no male slaves above the age of fourteen years; that they should "not buy knowingly any free Indian for a slave, nor make a slave of any Indian that ought to be free, that is to say, an Indian of any nation that is in amity and under the protection of this government"; and that they should not buy an Indian as slave until such had been at least three days in the town of the warrior who had captured him. Any Indian trader who, by his own confession or by verdict of a jury, should be found guilty of selling any free Indian as a slave, at any time after the ratification of this act, should forfeit the sum of £60 current money of the province, and failing to pay such fine, was to receive such corporal punishment as the judges of a General Session might decree, not extending to life or limb; and upon conviction for such offense the Indian slave so sold was declared free. The directions further urged the agents to aim constantly to promote peace and good will among all nations of Indians with whom South Carolina was accustomed to trade, and to engage as many others as possible to embrace the friendship and amity of the English.

In the enactment of these measures it was not the purpose of the assembly to stop the traffic in Indians, but only to regulate it by preventing the illegal acquisition of Indians by the traders and by requiring the traders to dispose of their Indians to the board itself which would then sell the Indians as it chose. Their action was dictated by a double purpose: to prevent the traders kidnapping Indians belonging to the tribes friendly to the colony and so bring on dangerous Indian uprisings; and to obtain the profits of the trade for the colonial exchequer, which not infrequently meant for their own profit. Humanitarian feeling for the Indians played no part in their action. The matter was made more complicated by the governor neglecting to sustain the action of the assembly. The explanation of his attitude is not difficult. He was accustomed to obtain substantial perquisites from the sale of Indians. Valuable gifts were presented him by the traders for allowing them to remain unmolested. On one occasion Governor Nathan Johnson refused £200 offered by the assembly for his Indian perquisites.

As already observed, the check on the traders by the creation of the board of commissioners was so slight that they continued as before to traffic in Indians with impunity. Unprincipled traders were licensed and obtained Indians wherever and however they could. Some traders went so far as to keep a body of slaves with them in the Indian nation where they traded, whom they sent out to attack other tribes for the purpose of obtaining captives. Attempts, of course, were made by the board to check the traffic. At its meetings Indian agents were tried for illegally reducing Indians to slavery, and on one occasion it was ordered that a woman and child should be brought back from New York where they had been sold as slaves. In 1711, an attempt was made to check the practice of the traders employing Indian slaves in the manner above mentioned, by issuing the following order to all traders: "You shall permit none of your slaves to go to war on any account whatsoever." This order had as little effect as those which preceded it. The influence of the traders, indeed, among the friendly tribes could accomplish the same result by stirring them up against other tribes.

These and other efforts at regulation of the Indian slave trade were alike fruitless. The general weakness of the province made it impossible to control the action of the traders on the frontier and outside the boundary of the province. Reports to the English Board of Trade made frequent mention of the state of affairs but conditions were not remedied. On October 27, 1720, several merchants suggested to the Board of Trade, as a means of improving conditions in South Carolina, "to prohibit by still greater penalties the selling as a slave of any person of the nations in amity with us throughout the continent and to prevent abuse therein" and declaring that "none but deputies from the public should have power to buy Indian slaves from those Indians in alliance with us as taken in war, which deputies on public account should be obliged to transfer them to the Islands there to be sold on condition not to be sent to the province again."

But the provincial authorities could not enforce these decrees, so the action of the traders continued unmolested until checked by other causes. Government officials continued to league with the traders. As late as 1754, a Catawba trader wrote to the board of commissioners as follows: "The Catawbas held a council yesterday in the king's house, and have resolved to go with the English against the French. They want me and my people to go with them, and we are willing to do so, even without pay, on one condition: that we be allowed to keep as our own property whatever plunder in the way of Indian slaves we may be able to capture." There are frequent intimations in the records that Indian slaves were still being held in South Carolina at this time, though their wholesale delivery and sale in Charleston had ceased.

In Virginia trade with the Indians began at an early date, and the traffic in Indians became later a part of it. The French reported, in 1701, that the English from Virginia, established among the Chickasaw, had armed the Savages with guns, joined with them in their expeditions against other people, especially the "Colipissas" (Acolapissa), and had sent the prisoners to be sold as slaves in the West Indies, keeping the children as slaves for themselves.

For some time the Virginia authorities did not recognize the right of the whites to enslave an Indian, no matter how obtained. In the session of 1657-1658, the assembly passed an act forbidding the stealing of Indian children or the buying of them from Indians or others for traffic, or the selling of them under any condition by the English, on penalty of 500 pounds of tobacco. In 1662, the assembly passed an act declaring that if any Englishman should bring in any Indians as servants and assign them to any one else he should not sell them as slaves or for any longer time than English servants of like age should serve by act of assembly. The assembly evidently intended to enforce these acts, for in the session of 1662 it ordered a Powhatan Indian to be freed who had been sold to the English by the chief of another tribe who, according to the assembly, had no right thus to sell him.

By 1670 the assembly appears to have modified in a measure its opinion regarding Indian slaves. An act of that year declared Indians taken in war by any other nation and sold by such nation to the English to be servants for life, if brought in by sea—if boys or girls, till thirty years old; if men or women, twelve years and no longer. By a later act of 1682 the legislature repealed the act of 1670 and definitely decided who should be slaves. Among those specified were all Indians obtained by purchase, in case they and their parents were not Christians at the time of their first being purchased by a Christian, although afterwards and before their importation into Virginia, they might have become converted to the Christian faith; and all Indians thereafter sold by the neighboring Indians or any other trafficking in slaves. But in 1691 these acts in turn were repealed and after that date no Indian could legally be bought or sold as a slave in Virginia.

Legislation, however, did not end the bringing of Indian slaves into the colony. Lawson records the sale in Virginia before 1700 of a young Indian woman brought from beyond the mountains. In 1715, the Carolina settlers reported to the home government that the Sarrow Indians were selling in Virginia among other commodities slaves (presumably Indian as well as negro) taken from the Carolina colonists.

Yet the Indian slaves brought into Virginia through the process of trade were never so numerous as in the Carolinas or the New England colonies, because the trade of Virginia with the Indian country was never so extensive as that of the Carolinas, or with the Carolinas so extensive as that of New England. Neither was the industry of the Virginia colonists in the early days such as to require

Indian slaves from the traders. The export trade was largely carried on with the mother country instead of with the colonies. The whole system of trade was not conducive to traffic in Indians.

In New England there was no direct traffic with the Indian tribes such as existed in the south. Instead, Indian slaves were obtained by trade with the other colonies, notably the Carolinas. Commerce of this sort, abundant evidence of which is furnished by the newspapers of the time, flourished from the opening of the eighteenth century until some time after the Tuscarora War.

In Massachusetts the number of Indians imported from the south increased so rapidly that the colonial authorities feared certain disastrous effects upon the colony from their presence. Accordingly, August 23, 1712, an act was passed, the preamble of which set forth four reasons for its enactment: the Indian slaves imported from the south were "malicious, surly and revengeful"; the industry of the colony was unlike that of the West Indies; with savage enemies at hand, it was dangerous to have bondsmen of a kindred race; the influx of the slaves discouraged the importation of Christian servants. Accordingly it was forbidden to import "any Indian, male or female, by land or sea from any part or place whatever, to be disposed of, sold or left within the province" on pain of forfeit to her Majesty's government, unless the offender "importing such Indians give security at the Secretary's office at £50 per head, to transport or carry out the same again within the space of one month next after their coming in, not to be returned back to this province." It was also provided that the captain or commander of any ship bringing such Indians into the province should, within twenty-four hours after the arrival of such ship, report the names, number and sex of such Indians, and give security of £50, under penalty of £50 for neglect to do so.

On December 28, 1725, Massachusetts passed an act regarding the exportation of Indians. This measure, like that of 1712, was not humanitarian but self-protective. The act forbade the carrying of any Indian out of the province except by legal authority, or on condition of giving £100 security for the safe return of such Indian, due allowance being made for unforeseen exigencies.

New Haven, also, in 1656, passed a general law ordering that no person should sell "any servant male or female of what degree soever" out of the colony unless into some of the other three colonies belonging to the New England Confederation, without leave and license from the authorities of that plantation to which such servant belonged, under penalty of a fine of £10 for each offense. The measure could be applied to Indian slaves, though not intended specifically for that purpose.

After the Tuscarora War the importation of "revengeful, warlike savages" alarmed the Connecticut colonists and led to definite legislative action regarding the matter. In view of the fact that several persons had brought into the colony Carolina Indians, "which have committed many cruel and bloody outrages" there, and "may draw off our Indians" to the extent of arousing hostilities if their importation were continued, in July, 1715, the governor and council decided to prohibit the importation of Indian slaves until the meeting of the assembly, and to require each ship entering port with Indians on board to give a bond of £50 to remove them from the colony within twenty days. Further they decided that Indians brought into the colony thereafter should be "kept in strictest custody" and "prevented from communicating with other Indians" unless the owner gave the same bond as above to take them out of the colony within twenty days.'

The following October, the general court, copying the Massachusetts act of 1712, made permanent the prohibition to import Indian slaves, since "divers conspiracies, outrages, barbarities, murders, burglaries, thefts, and other notorious crimes at sundry times, and especially of late, have been perpetrated by Indians and other slaves, . . . being of a malicious and vengeful spirit, rude and insolent in their behavior, and very ungovernable, the overgreat number of which, considering the different circumstances in this colony from the plantations in the islands and our having considerable numbers of Indians, natives of our country, may be of pernicious consequence." An act was then passed decreeing the forfeiture of all Indians thereafter imported, and the payment of a fine of £50 by the shipmaster or any other person who might bring them. Since this act did not stop the importation, another was enacted in 1750 providing that "all Indians, male or female, of what age soever, imported or brought into this colony by sea or land, from any place whatever, to be disposed of, left or sold within this colony, shall be forfeited to the treasury of this colony, and may be seized and taken accordingly; unless the person or persons importing or bringing in such Indian or Indians shall give security to some naval officer of this colony of £50 per head, to transport or carry out of the same again, within the space of one month after their coming, not to be returned back again to this colony."

A similar act passed in 1774 forbade the importation of Indian, negro or mulatto slaves. The act stated that the cause of this legislation was the fact that the "increase of slaves in this colony is injurious to the poor and inconvenient." Any person, therefore, importing Indian, negro or mulatto slaves or knowingly bringing them as such, should forfeit to the treasurer of the colony the sum of £100 for each slave so imported or purchased.

Rhode Island, in August, 1676, decreed that any person importing Indians into the colony without permission of the colonial authorities, should forfeit all right to them and pay a fine of £5 to the colony. Certain persons allowed to import such Indians were directed to pay half the sum of the sale to the treasurer or forfeit the Indians; and all persons were forbidden to carry any Indians out of the colony without permission of the government, under penalty of £5.

As a special measure of protection against internal disturbances, the general assembly of Rhode Island, also, passed an act, January 4, 1704, forbidding, under penalty of forfeiture, the importation of Indians either to be kept or sold. And if any person brought Indians into the colony and set them at liberty under the pretense of bringing them as servants, such person would have to carry such Indians out of the colony at his own expense. If the person importing Indians failed to remove them, he should be seized by the authorities and dealt with according to law, as should also the person having them in his possession.

The Indian wars in the southern colonies brought the same action in Rhode Island as in the other New England colonies. In July 5, 1715, an act was passed to prohibit the importation of Indian slaves. The preamble of the act States that in both Rhode Island and the neighboring colonies, "conspiracies, insurrections, rapes, thefts and other execrable crimes" had been perpetrated by the Indian slaves, "and the increase of them in this colony daily discourages the importing of white servants from Great Britain, etc., into this colony, which if not immediately remedied may prove very pernicious and troublesome to this government." The act, therefore, provided that within three months after its publication, all Indians, male or female, of whatever age, brought by land or sea, from any part or place, to be disposed of, sold or left within the colony, should be forfeited to his majesty, for and toward the support of the colony, unless the person who brought in such Indian or Indians, should give security of £50 per head to carry them out within the period of one month. All masters of ships, and others engaged in the traffic, were to record in the secretary's office within twenty-four hours after arrival the names, number and sex of the Indians and give security of £50 per head. Failure to meet this requirement was to be punished by the confiscation of the Indians. This act was continued in force and was reënacted in the Digest of Laws in 1766.

In New Hampshire a law was passed in 1714 forbidding the importation or bringing into the province, by sea or land, of any male or female Indian to be used as a servant or a slave. This was done because of the fact that "notorious crimes or enormities have of late been perpetrated and committed by Indians or other slaves, within several of her Majesty's plantations in America" and because the use of Indian slaves was considered "a discouragement to Christian servants." By the terms of the act, "Indians, male or female, of what age soever, that shall be imported or brought into this province by sea or land, every master of ship or other vessel, merchant or person, importing or bringing into this province such Indians, male or female, shall forfeit to her Majesty, for the support of the government, the sum of £10 per head, to be sued for and recovered in any of her Majesty's courts of record, . . . to be paid into the treasury for the use of the aforesaid." The occasion for this act was the same as that for the Massachusetts act of 1712, namely, the bringing of southern Indian slaves to the northern colonies. The influence of Massachusetts is readily seen, for Indian slaves could not have been so numerous as to have been a serious menace in a province of fewer than 10,000 inhabitants.

A part of the small number of Indian slaves in the colony of New York came through the process of trade. Indians from the Carolinas, for example, were sold there. Since New York took certain legislative action regarding other Indians but never considered the importation of the southern Indians, it may be concluded that the number imported during the southern wars was never sufficiently large to cause any concern in the colony. Probably very few, if any, came into the colony through direct trade with the Indians themselves.

Though the number of Indians imported into Pennsylvania was also small, it was large enough to lead to legislation concerning it. January 12, 1706, the general assembly passed an act to prevent the importation of Indian slaves from any other province or colony of America after March 25, 1706. The preamble of the act stated that the importation of Indians from Carolina and other places had given offense to the Indians of the province and caused them to become suspicious and dissatisfied. Perhaps a fellow feeling, or perhaps the fear that the custom of the whites using Indian slaves might affect their liberty, led the Indians, already in a state of disturbance, to protest against such importation. At the same time, the act declared "that no such Indian slave, as deserting his master's service elsewhere shall fly into this province, shall be understood or construed to be comprehended within this act." A further exception was made in the case of those slaves with their children who, for the space of one year before such importation, could be proved to have been menial servants in the family of the importer. Any slave brought into the province contrary to this law was declared forfeited to the government, and was to be set free or otherwise disposed of according to the will of the governor and council.

The law of 1706 proved to be inadequate. The continued importation of Indians and the still existing fear of having ungovernable and dangerous slaves in the colony, led to the passage in 1712 of a second act, already mentioned, which levied a duty of £20 on every negro or Indian imported. Masters of vessels bringing them in were required to state their number and the name of the importer. Any negro or Indian in whose case these provisions were violated was to be seized and sold by provincial officers, and the money obtained from their sale paid to the treasurer for the use of the government. Duties paid upon any negro or Indian imported, but exported again within twenty days, however, were to be returned. One

Samuel Holt was appointed to put the act into execution, and was given the necessary powers to use force, if necessary, to find concealed negroes and Indians whose owners had not complied with the terms of the act, and to dispose in public sale of those so captured. Owners could bring back their runaway negro or Indian slaves, and "gentlemen and strangers" traveling in the province were allowed to retain their negro or Indian slaves for a time not exceeding six months. But the act was not put into operation, for it was repealed by the queen in council, February 20, 1714.

INDIAN SLAVERY

CHAPTER VIII. OTHER PROCESSES of ENSLAVEMENT

IT sometimes happened that the Indians sold to the whites, for a specified number of years, members of their own tribe as a punishment for some grievous offense. Families sold some of their own members into temporary servitude to obtain money or other necessities or an individual Indian offered himself or his children as security for loans, and, on failure to meet the obligations, became the slaves of the creditors. Occasionally an outcast or disgraced Indian, having lost his position in the family or the tribe, sold himself into slavery to the whites in order to escape punishment at the hands of his own people and to secure future protection for himself.

The treachery of the whites in refusing to give up the Indians at the expiration of the specified term of service, and the selling of them out of the country, caused considerable disturbance among the Indians in several colonies. In 1660, a company of English from Massachusetts settled on Old Town Creek at its junction with Cape Fear River in the present North Carolina. The settlement was short lived, lasting something less than three years. One reason why the settlers left was the hostile attitude of neighboring Indians who believed that the white men had shipped off as slaves some of the Indian children who had been entrusted to their care, under the pretext of sending them north to be educated. Though the charge has never been substantiated, it seems probable that it was not without cause. The lax state of morals among the early settlers would permit the kidnapping of Indians to be practiced by this little settlement as well as elsewhere. But whether the settlers were guilty or not on this particular occasion, the incident throws a certain light on the custom of the times through the fear which the Indians showed of such treatment. Evidently the practice continued in North Carolina, for one of the grievances of the Tuscarora Indians at the breaking out of the Tuscarora War was that their children who had been bound out for a limited time in English families, were, contrary to the spirit of the agreement, transported to other plantations and sold as slaves.

Virginia was always comparatively lenient in her treatment of the Indians. Accordingly, its early legislation dealt with the matter of unjustly forcing Indians into slavery. In 1655, provision was made that Indian children could become indentured servants only by consent of their parents and for specified terms agreed upon, and such children were to be educated in the Christian religion. The following year, 1656, it was provided that Indian children brought into the colony as hostages should be assigned to masters by choice of their parents, but should not be made slaves. Again, in 1658, it was decreed that any Indian children disposed of by their parents to a white man for "education and instruction in the Christian religion" or for any other purpose, were not to be turned over to any other person upon any pretext whatever, and any such child was to be free at the age of twenty-five. The fact that the legislation on the subject was repeated at such short intervals affords evidence of the continuance of the custom which it was intended to abolish. A letter of Governor Spotswood to Lord Dartmouth, March 11, 1711, regarding the Indian college, tells of his attempt to persuade Indians to allow their children to attend the college by remitting their annual tribute of skins, and declares that "they were a little shy of yielding to his proposal, and urged the breach of a former contract made long ago by this government, when instead of their children receiving the promised education, they were transported, as they say, to other countries and sold as slaves."

Massachusetts sought to control the custom of the Indians in apprenticing themselves and their children to the whites and the consequent abuse of the practice, by enacting, in 1700, a law requiring the consent of two or more justices of the peace to such a proceeding, so as to make sure that the terms of the agreement were reasonable. The justices of the regular courts were empowered to hear the complaint of an Indian with regard to any indenture or apprenticeship, and to settle the matter. Similar acts were passed in 1718 and 1725. The latter act provided a heavy fine for taking any children beyond the seas without due legal sanction, and further decreed that any indenture then existing of an adult Indian should be good for no longer than one year from the date of the passage of the law, except by legal approval as specified in the law. In 1763, another act, to continue as law for three years, was passed, forbidding any Marshpee Indian to bind out his or her child or children to any English person whatsoever by indenture or any other way, in satisfaction of or as security for a debt, without the consent of the major part of the overseers, and declaring that every indenture or any instrument whatever, or oral agreement whereby such child or children should be bound out contrary to the true intent and meaning of the act, should be adjudged null and Void.

Rhode Island, also, for the same purpose of preventing the conversion of apprenticeship into actual slavery, passed an act, June 15, 1730, requiring the assent of two justices to any bond of apprenticeship to which the Indians were parties. If the Indian captives disposed of for periods of years by Rhode Island at the close of King Philip's War are to be considered as involuntary indentured servants, then such abuses as the law of 1730 were intended to remedy existed with reference to those captives. By the terms of their disposal they were to be free after a temporary period of service. But the colonists sometimes continued to hold them in servitude after the specified term had expired. Furthermore, though no provision for such action was made by the colonial government, the masters of these servants held as slaves the children born of these Indians while in servitude.

Conditions in New York in the eighteenth century serve to illustrate the same point. In July, 1715, Colonel Heathcote wrote home to Secretary Townsend: "The Indians complain that their children, who were many of them bound out for a limited time to be taught and instructed by the Christians, were, contrary to the intent of their agreement, transferred to other plantations and sold for slaves, and I don't know but there may be some truth in what they allege." The authorities were aware of the danger caused by the colonists' action, and in 1750 Governor Clinton ordered all Indian children held as pledges or slaves, to be returned to their families. Johnson, the Indian commissioner, was much pleased with the governor's action and January 22, 1750, wrote him: "I am very glad that your excellency has given orders to have the Indian children returned, who are kept by the traders as pawns or pledges as they call it, but rather stolen from them (as the parents came at the appointed time to redeem them, but they sent them away before hand), and as they were children of our Friends and Allies, and if they are not returned next Spring, it will confirm what the French told the Six Nations (viz.): that we looked upon them as slaves or negroes, which affair gave me a great deal of trouble at that time to reconcile." Evidently the holders were disinclined to obey the governor's order, for Johnson cited in his letter two cases where such return had not been made, and from which he feared disturbance. To what extent the governor's decree was effective would be hard to state. There certainly were Indian slaves in the colony after its publication.

"A list of the Negro, Indian and Mulatto Slaves within the district whereof Benjamin Smith is Captain at Hempstead in Queens County taken the first day of April, 1755,"shows that Indian slaves were being used on Long Island at that date, and it seems not unlikely that some of them might have been obtained by abuse of indenture.

Another process of enslaving Indians was that which had to do with the infliction of punishment for offenses against law and order. The custom of sentencing Indians to enslavement at home, or to transportation and enslavement abroad, for such offenses was general throughout the colonies. Such a sentence came about in one of two ways: either the colonial legislature enacted a law which imposed enslavement as the punishment for a given offense; or a colonial court acting on its own initiative used it to that end.

In South Carolina, even after the wholesale deportation of captive and kidnapped Indians for slaves had practically ceased, natives were sometimes sentenced to slavery by the assembly as punishment for crime of which the accused was convicted or suspected. Such an instance occurred, May 29, 1725, when it was "Ordered that Colonel Alexander Parris, Public Receiver, do forthwith sell the Indian now in jail for the supposed murder of a white man to the northward of the province, in order that he may be transferred to Bermuda, Jamaica or Barbadoes, or some other of the West India Islands." Again on May 31, 1732,

"His Excellency having asked the advice of the Council in relation to an Indian delivered up by her own nation, now in jail of this town, on suspicion of having murdered an Indian trader; it is resolved, that as it could not be fully proved that she was the person that murdered the said Indian trader, but strong presumptions appearing ordered that Colonel Parris cause her to be transported and sold, for the use of the Publick." A similar instance occurred in Massachusetts in 1666 when the general court sentenced a Pequot to slavery for life as punishment for the murder of a white colonist by the Indians.

In Virginia, as a measure of protection to property rights upon a complaint of damages committed by Indians, the assembly voted in 1660 that the plaintiff in the case be given the right, provided satisfaction were not made, to sell as many Indians out of the country as the court might prescribe. Another act of similar character was passed in 1722 after the treaty of Albany, when the assembly voted that no Virginia Indian should cross the Potomac River, and that none of the Five Nations or their allies should go beyond that boundary. Any offenders were to be punished by death, or be transported and sold as slaves. In Massachusetts, also, the question of runaway slaves who sought refuge among the Indians, led the general court, June 2, 1641, to pass an order by which it was declared to be the mind of the court "that if the Indians send not back our runaways, then, by commission of the governor and any three of the magistrates, to send and take so many as to satisfy for the want of them and for the charge of sending for them." The order, like that of the Virginia legislature, meant that any master might be authorized to right himself upon the Indians for wrong done him by them.

Not only the higher courts, but the lower courts as well, were accustomed to make use of this form of punishment. In 1678, the court of Sandwich, Plymouth, directed that three Indians convicted of breaking open a house and stealing therefrom, should be perpetual slaves, and empowered the owner of the house and stolen property to "make sale of them in New England or elsewhere, as his lawful slaves. for the term of their lives."

Their love of strong drink not infrequently led the Indians into temporary servitude, and served as a means by which the colonists, if so minded, could force them into that condition. On one occasion Boston was building a fort on an island in the harbor. Wages were high and economy was desirable. The general court, therefore, ordered that for drunkenness the Indians should not be whipped, but sent to this island to work for ten days. The Indians protested and preferred whipping as punishment, but their complaint received no attention.

On March 8, 1683, the Plymouth general court decreed that a certain Indian should serve as a slave for a specified time because of a judgment against him. At a council held in Boston, also, June 14, 1686, upon notification of the keeper of the prison that a sentence of transportation of an Indian had not been carried into effect, the treasurer was ordered to sell the Indian for a period not exceeding seven years in satisfaction of the judgment against him. The Massachusetts council records of January 18, 1695, tell of an Indian accused of "corresponding with and adhering to the Indian enemy" who was transported and sold for the offense. A similar instance occurred in 1696, when an Indian was condemned "to be transported beyond the seas as a dangerous person and sold." On December 1, 1705, the Massachusetts deputies sent in a bill providing that fornication or marriage of white men with negroes or Indians should be punished by selling the colored offenders out of the colony as slaves. Through the intercession of Samuel Sewall, the Indians were dropped from the bill which was then passed as applying to blacks and mulattoes. The records mention other instances in 1713 and 1776 when Indians were sold as punishment for crime, the latter case being one of theft. An incident occurred in 1721 when the sentence of an Indian imprisoned in Boston was changed from imprisonment to a term of Servitude. Another Indian, in 1727, was sold for a term of years to a resident of the colony to serve a sentence for debt. In 1739, on petition of the sheriff of Barnstaple county, the Massachusetts general court impowered the justices of that county to sell an Indian prisoner convicted of manslaughter and sentenced to imprisonment "to any of his majesty's good subjects for a term not exceeding ten years, for the most he will fetch in order to get money to pay the cost of prosecuting the prisoner and the charges of his imprisonment."

The Indians of Rhode Island gave much trouble by stealing the goods and cattle of the colonists. To prevent it, a law was passed, 1659, to the effect that, if the damage exceeded twenty shillings, the convict might be sold as a slave to any English plantation abroad unless he made restitution. Instances are not lacking in which the law of 1659 was put into effect. On one occasion (between 1671 and 1685) an Indian convicted of breaking into a house and of beating and wounding a servant, was sentenced to pay a fine, or, if payment were not made in three months, to be sold as a slave in Barbadoes. In 1676, the general court provided that all Indians who should come upon any island in the bay, must have written permission so to do from the committee appointed to dispose of Indians, without which they would be liable to be sold into servitude.

The first code of Connecticut laws, 1650, followed the Massachusetts Body of Liberties in authorizing enslavement as a mode of punishment. In 1650, certain Indians who failed to make satisfaction for injuries were ordered to be seized and delivered to the injured party, "either to serve or to be shipped out . . . as the case will justly bear." In 1660, the general court was empowered by the United Colonies to send a company of men to obtain satisfaction from the Narraganset for certain depredations upon the settlers. Four of the guilty Indians were to be demanded and sent to Barbadoes to be sold as slaves.

Not only did the New England colonies take separately such legislative action regarding the enslavement of Indians, but Plymouth, Massachusetts, Connecticut, and New Haven acting together as the New England Confederation, took similar action. Alleged trespassing of Indians upon English territory, and the fear of a Narraganset war, led the United Colonies, in 1646, to pass an order authorizing, upon complaint of trespass by Indians, the seizure of any of them who should "entertain, protect or rescue the offender."

"And because it will be chargeable keeping Indians in prison, and if they should escape, they are like to prove more insolent and dangerous after, that upon such seizure, the delinquent or satisfaction be demanded of the sagamore or plantation of Indians guilty or accessory as before, and if it be denied, that the magistrates of the jurisdiction deliver up the Indians seized to the party or parties indamaged, either to serve or to be shipped out in exchange for negroes as the case will justly bear." The commissioners agreed that this measure, though just, was severe, and that it might lead to the Indians seizing the English in return; but they could see no better means of preserving the peace of the colony. As a measure of fairness, therefore, they decreed that before any seizure of Indians was made, a copy of the declaration should be published and given to the particular sagamore. Copies were accordingly given to four leading sachems.

A further process of enslavement was connected with questions of birth. By the recognized common law of nations, the civil law and the Jewish law, the children of a slave mother became at birth the property of the mother's owner. Nobody thought of the children of slaves being free. Yet, to make certainty doubly sure, the colonial laws from time to time considered the matter and declared the common law a part of colonial legislation. South Carolina, for example, by an act of 1712, repeated in 1722, and 1735, declared that, "with the exception of certain individuals freed by the government, all negroes, mulattoes, mustizoes, or Indians which at any time heretofore haye been sold, or now are held or taken to be, or hereafter shall be bought and sold as slaves, are hereby declared slaves; and they and their children, are hereby made and declared slaves to all intents and purposes." Another act of 1740, though worded differently, decreed a similar condition for the children of negro, mulatto, mustee and Indian slave mothers. In 1705, Virginia similarly declared all children bond or free according to the condition of their mothers; and, in 1723, decreed that children of female mulattoes or Indians obliged by law to serve till the age of thirty or thirty-one should serve the master or mistress of such mulatto or Indian until they should attain the same age as that up to which the mother was obliged by law to serve.

A Maryland act of 1663 differs from the acts just mentioned by stating that "all children born of any negro or other slave, shall be slaves as their fathers were for the term of their lives." Another section of this same act provides that "whatsoever freeborn woman shall intermarry with any slave, from and after the last day of the present assembly, shall serve the master of such slave during the life of her husband; and that all the issue of such freeborn woman, so married, shall be slaves as their fathers were." Though the law was of brief duration, persons born of the union between slaves and free white women, and the descendants of such persons, were held in slavery down to 1791, when the highest court of the state decided that for want of proof concerning the white woman who originally married a slave, her descendants were not slaves, and could not be legally held as such. A later Maryland act, June 2, 1692, provided that all children born or thereafter to be born of slaves within the province were to be slaves for the term of their natural lives. Nothing is said in the act of children one of whose parents was free. The act was repealed in 1715. New York, on its own part, in 1706, decreed that any negro, Indian, mulatto or mustee child should follow the condition of the mother and be esteemed a slave "to all intents and purposes whatsoever." Frequent incidental mention, also, is found in the documents of the time and in newspaper advertisements to slaves "born in the house."

Certain judicial decisions rendered in the trial of cases in federal and state courts, finally, offer clear indication as to the legality of holding in slavery the children of Indian slave mothers. Of these decisions the one rendered by the Virginia court of appeals in 1831 is particularly instructive. In part it runs as follows: "I cannot for a moment doubt the propriety of the former decisions of this court, and of the instructions under consideration, that proof that a party is descended in the female line from an Indian woman, and especially a native American, without anything more is *prima facie* proof of his right to freedom liable to be repelled by proof that his race has been immemorially held in slavery; which may be in turn rebutted by the consideration of the ignorance and helpless condition of persons in that situation, aided by other circumstances, such as that many such were bound by law to a service equivalent, in all respects, to a state of temporary slavery, until they attained the age of thirty-one years; and in many cases (according to circumstances existing in almost every case) for an uncertain term beyond that age."

INDIAN SLAVERY

CHAPTER IX. PROPERTY RELATIONS

Though the practices connected with the institution of negro and Indian slavery in the Spanish colonies were known to the English colonists, yet at first the latter did not see fit to impose the status of slavery upon the Indians brought into the colonies by way of trade with the Spanish islands or otherwise, but were content to retain possession of the services of their subject Indians without taking possession of their persons through legal declarations imposing the status of slavery upon them. Such Indians were held in the status of servitude, a condition which stood "midway between freedom and absolute subjection" and which was the "historic base upon which slavery, by the extension and addition of incidents, was constructed." The right of ownership of the services of both negroes and Indians was, after all, what the colonists most desired, and appeared to promise satisfaction in this instance as it had in the case of the white indentured servants. Indian servitude not only preceded Indian slavery, but even continued after the institution of slavery was fully developed. This is true of most, if not all, of the English-American colonies. It is certainly true of Maryland, Massachusetts, Rhode Island, Pennsylvania, Georgia, North Carolina and South Carolina. Statutory recognition of slavery in general by the English-American colonies occurred as follows: by Massachusetts in 1641; by Connecticut in 1650; by Virginia in 1661; by Maryland in 1663; by New York and New Jersey in 1664; by South Carolina in 1682; by Pennsylvania and Rhode Island in 1700; by North Carolina in 1715; and by Georgia in 1755. But the legislation of these dates did not always include the subject Indians. When such was the case, however, according to a strict legal interpretation, any subject Indian, if enslaved, had the right to demand his freedom from the colonial courts. Such an instance existed in the case of Virginia where the acts of 1655 and 1661 specifically forbade Indian slavery and guaranteed to the subject Indians all the rights of servants.

The recognition of Indian as well as negro slavery by customary law came somewhat earlier than by statute law. With the extension of the period of servitude to a life term, the change from servitude to slavery was practically completed so far as customary law was concerned. Only the enactment of legal provisions sanctioning the change was necessary to complete the process. The common use in subsequent law of the terms "servant for life," "perpetual servant," and "bond servant" as synonymous with the term "slave" shows how little change was really effected in the condition of the servant. Such change consisted chiefly, from the standpoint of the master, in the extension of his right to service, and consequently in the extension of his obligation of protection and maintenance, and what was still more important, in the acquisition of the right of possession of the offspring of his slaves. From the standpoint of the slave, it meant little more than the loss of the right to ultimate liberty, political and civil, and the extension of his right to protection and maintenance.

The legislation which marked the changing status varied in nature in the several colonies. In certain colonies the slavery status was simply recognized as being in existence by certain acts relating to slaves, without any formal declaration to the effect that Indians held in servitude should be considered slaves. In other colonies the condition of slavery as applied to Indians was legalized by general acts relating to slavery in general, and not specifying either Indians or negroes. In still other colonies the holding of Indians in a condition of actual slavery was legalized by legislative acts relating directly to Indians. An act of this latter character was passed by New York in 1678 declaring that all Indians that should come to, or be brought into the province at any time during the succeeding six months, should be sold as slaves for the benefit of the government. South Carolina, in an act of 1712 relating to the "better ordering and governing of negroes and slaves" provided that "all negroes, mulattoes, mestizoes or Indians which have at any time heretofore been sold, or now are held and taken to be, or hereafter shall be brought and sold as slaves, are hereby declared slaves to all intents and purposes; excepting all such negroes, mulattoes, mestizoes or Indians which heretofore have been, or hereafter shall be for some particular merit, made and declared free, either by the Governor and Council of this province, or by their respective owners and masters; and also, excepting all such negroes, mulattoes, mestizoes or Indians as can prove they ought not to be sold as slaves." The acts, already mentioned in other connections, authorizing the enslavement of Indian captives taken in war, the holding in slavery of such captives when obtained in trade from sources outside the colony, and the enslavement of free Indians by the colonial authorities as punishment for misdemeanors and crimes, are also cases in point.

From the standpoint of English law the action of the colonial legislatures enacting the slavery status had no legal sanction. It was based on the interpretation of the common law of nations, that is, it was carried on in accordance with a "law not promulgated by legislation, and rested upon prevalent views of universal jurisprudence, or the law of nations supported by the express or implied authority of the home government concerning the institution of slavery." So the colonies, by a gradual process of changing conditions and legal enactments, substituted the slavery status for the servitude status without molestation from the home government, which was interested in colonial slave conditions and legislation only when the African slave trade was involved. So long, therefore, as the enactment of colonial laws decreeing the slavery status did not interfere with that trade, the home government gave no attention to the matter. As for Indian slavery *per se,* if England had given it any attention whatever, she would probably have considered it a purely colonial matter. Since it was never sufficiently extensive to interfere with negro slavery and the slave trade, it never received any attention from the home government, and so existed as legal because never declared illegal. An authority on the legal status of early American slavery states: "It may be laid down as a legal axiom, that in all governments in which the municipal regulations are not absolutely opposed to slavery, persons already reduced to that state may be held in it, and we also assume, as a first principle, that slavery has been permitted and tolerated in all the colonies established in America by European powers, as relates to blacks and also as relates to Indians in the first periods of conquest and colonization. This accounts in a measure for the absence of any legislative act of European powers for intruding slavery into the American dominions." Hence it followed that the English colonial charters authorizing the colonial legislatures to make laws, gave no license as such to enslave.

With the change from the status of servitude to the status of slavery, certain of the attributes of the former condition were continued and connected with the latter. Chief of these, and the fundamental idea on which the change was effected, was the conception of property right which, from the idea of the ownership of an individual's service resting upon contract implied or expressed, came to be that of the ownership of an individual's person.

Indian slaves were recognized as property in all the English colonies, and were openly bought and sold at both public and private sales like negroes and other property. They were advertised in the colonial newspapers with statements of their qualifications and ability for work, their ages, and sometimes descriptions of their personal appearance. From the New England newspapers it is apparent that for a time dealers advertised such slaves for sale openly in their own names. Later the possible purchaser was directed by the advertisement to "inquire of the Printer and know further" or to "inquire at the Post Office." It was not uncommon for slaves offered for sale to choose their future owner from those who desired to purchase them, or to approve the bill of sale.

Like other property, real or personal, Indian slaves could be given away by word of mouth or by "last will and testament.". One of the earliest of such wills on record is that of Governor John Winthrop of Massachusetts, made in 1639, by which he gave to his son Adam, Governor's Island and with it "also my Indians thereon." In South Carolina where Indian slaves were most numerous, the records of their disposal by will are frequent. The custom, in fact, was universal in the colonies.

Indian slaves were listed in the various colonies in the inventories of estates along with indentured servants of unexpired terms and negro slaves. They were taken like other chattels in payment for debt, and in certain of the colonies provision was made by law regarding the matter. South Carolina, February 7, 1690, decreed that a slave was to be taken like any other chattel as payment for debt. Maryland, 1729, passed an act to the effect that no slave should be taken for any debt due from the deceased so long as there should be any other goods sufficient for the purpose. In those colonies where legislation makes no mention of the matter, it is known from the history of negro slavery that the custom was similar to that of Carolina.

The proximity of the Indian tribes to the colonists, furthermore, afforded a condition most suitable for the escape of Indian slaves.

Individual testimony, frequent advertisements in the colonial newspapers giving descriptions of fugitive Indian slaves and offering rewards for their capture and return, and the amount of colonial legislation concerning both negro and Indian runaway slaves, show that Indians held in servitude took frequent advantage of the opportunities at hand for their escape, and that their owners used all possible means to regain their lost property. At the time following the Pequot War, Mason complained of the tendency to run away shown by the Pequot slaves in the colonies. The Indians enslaved after King Philip's War likewise escaped. Mayhew tells of runaway Indian slaves in Massachusetts in 1690. In this same year one Isaac Morrill of New Jersey was arrested at Newbury, Massachusetts, for enticing Indian and negro slaves to run away.

The *Boston News Letter* came into existence, 1704, at about the time when Indian slaves began to be brought into the northern colonies from the Spanish islands and from the Carolinas. Rarely was there an issue of that or the other Massachusetts newspapers from that time down to the Revolutionary period which did not contain an advertisement for a runaway Indian slave. Sometimes the same advertisement was repeated in two or three successive issues and was often inserted in more than one newspaper. For the capture and return of the fugitives, rewards were offered, sometimes indefinite in nature as "suitable rewards." These advertisements relate for the most part to fugitive men and boy Indian slaves, but advertisements relating to runaway women Indian slaves are not lacking. The escapes appear for the most part, though not always, to have been made singly. One advertisement shows two Indian men, two Indian women and an Indian boy belonging to different persons to have escaped together. Captains of vessels were often cautioned in the advertisements against carrying away such fugitive slaves, and any person harboring them or aiding them to escape was threatened with full penalty of the law.

All the colonies enacted fugitive slave laws. Some of these laws were applied to slaves in general, some to negroes and "other slaves," still others to negro, mulatto and Indian slaves. The colonies where slavery was of greatest extent had the most extensive and elaborate laws on the subject, and those colonies where Indian slavery existed to any considerable extent included the term "Indian slaves" in their laws. Pennsylvania made but little provision regarding runaway slaves. Maryland concerned itself more largely with servants.

Some of these laws did not define the term "runaway slave." Others in an attempt to avoid confusion gave clear explanations of the term. Such an act was passed by Connecticut in 1690, specifying that any Indian, mulatto or negro servants and slaves wandering outside the place to which they belonged without a ticket of leave or pass in writing from some assistant or justice of the peace or from their owner, were to be considered runaways and treated as such. New Jersey, in 1713, considered as runaways any negro, mulatto or Indian slave who was five miles from his master's habitation without written leave of absence from his owner, and any such slave found in New Jersey but belonging to another province was declared a runaway. South Carolina, by the act of 1690, considered as a runaway any negro or Indian slave absent from his master's plantation (no distance specified), without a written ticket of leave unless in company with a white man.

To discourage aid and assistance being given fugitive slaves, the colonies specified by legislative acts the punishment to follow such offense. On June 14, 1705, Lord Cornbury, in his opening speech to the New York assembly, expressed his opinion regarding the necessity for passing an act to prevent negro, Indian and mulatto slaves running away from their masters. An act of the common council of Albany, 1686, forbade all persons harboring negro or Indian slaves in their houses without the owners' consent. Pennsylvania, 1726, decreed a fine of five shillings for the first hour and one shilling for every hour afterward that any person should harbor or entertain any runaway negro, Indian or mulatto slave. Virginia, by the act of 1705, specified a fine of £100 for any shipmaster transporting any negro, mulatto or Indian slave out of the colony without permission of the owner. South Carolina, also, by an act of 1690, levied forty shillings fine on any one not attempting to apprehend a negro or Indian slave coming into his plantation without a ticket of leave from his master or not accompanied by a white man.

Not infrequently the colonial authorities were called upon to furnish protection to the owners of Indian slaves against their seizure by the free Indians, or against fugitive Indian slaves being hidden and retained by the tribes. To effect the return of such slaves special inducements were offered by the colonial government from time to time. At the close of the Pequot War an agreement was made by the chief, Miantonomo, and the Massachusetts government, by which the former promised to seize such Pequot slaves as escaped, and return them to their owners. On June 2, 1641, the general court of Massachusetts made a similar agreement with Lieutenant Willard of Concord, Ensign Holman of Dorchester, and Sergeant Collacot of Dorchester. As a partial return for the monopoly of the Indian trade granted them, these men agreed to demand, wherever they should find them, all fugitive Pequot slaves that belonged to the English. A similar request for protection is found in New York, where two widows petitioned governor and council, May 16, 1717, regarding two Indian slaves who were secreted by the Indians of Pekkemeck. Events in North Carolina, following the Tuscarora War, offer numerous illustrations of colonial action taken to secure the return of such fugitives. The Indian slaves in the colony, consisting largely of the captive Tuscarora, frequently escaped and took refuge with the free Indians of their tribe. The Indians neglected to return these runaways, and the council was compelled to call many times upon "King Blount" to compel his people to return the slaves according to his agreement with the Carolina government. Such action is recorded as late as 1731.

Sometimes this protection of slave owners in their property rights assumed intercolonial importance. Such a recognition of property rights occurred in the articles of federation of the United Colonies of New England, 1643, in the provision: "If any servant run away from his master into any of these confederated jurisdictions, . . . in such case, upon certificate of one magistrate in the jurisdiction of which the said servant fled, or upon other due proof, the said servant shall be delivered, either to his master or any other that pursues and brings such certificate or proof."

Since it was found that certain Indian villages harbored fugitive Indians, the Confederation, September 5, 1646, decided that such villages might be raided and the inhabitants carried off, women and children being spared as far as possible, and declared that "because it will be chargeable keeping Indians in prison and, if they should escape, they are liable to prove more insolent and dangerous after, it was thought fit that upon such seizure . . . the magistrates of the jurisdiction deliver up the Indian seized to the party or parties indamaged, either to serve or to be shipped out and exchanged for negroes, as the cause will justly bear." In the same year the commissioners of the United Colonies sent a letter to Governor Kieft of New Netherland demanding the return of an Indian captive "fled from her master at Hartford" and "entertained in your house at Hartford and, though required by the magistrate, . . . under the hands of your agent there denied . . . and said to have been either married or abused by one of your men." "Such a servant," they declared, "is part of her master's estate and a more considerable part than a beast." Kieft refused to give up the Indian woman, and replied: "as concerns the barbarian handmaid" it is "apprehended by Some, that she is no slave, but a freewoman, because she was neither taken in war, nor bought with price, but was in former times placed with me by her parents for education." By the intercolonial treaty of September 19, 1650, the provision of the articles of confederation concerning fugitive slaves was extended so as to include the intercourse of the New Englanders and the Dutch. Another fugitive slave law similar to that of 1643 was contained in the articles of confederation of the United Colonies in 1672.

Similar events involved New York and Pennsylvania. In 1723, some Seneca Indians trading in South Carolina carried away an Indian slave boy belonging to an Englishman there. The governor of New York charged the Seneca with the act and demanded that the slave boy be returned. The Seneca acknowledged that they were among the party who took the slave boy, said that he had been given to some Susquehanna Indians, and requested the governor to ask for him there. An undated letter of William Penn to the Susquehanna Indians regarding some Indian slaves taken from the people of New York by them, refers to a similar incident. In it Penn mentions the people of New York having twice appealed to him regarding an Indian woman and boy, both slaves, bought in New York from the governor of Carolina, which the Susquehanna Indians had taken away. Penn urged the Susquehanna to deliver the slaves to his messenger that they might be put on board a vessel and returned to New York.

In July, 1682, Plymouth provided that if any Indian who was a servant of the English should run away, "such Indians where such a runaway Indian is come, shall forthwith give notice of the runaway to the Indian constable, who shall immediately apprehend such Indian servant and carry him or her before the overseer or next magistrate."

At a meeting, January 9, 1713, the council of North Carolina considered the matter of two Indian slaves sent to the colony from Virginia, and found that they belonged to two residents of South Carolina from whom, presumably, they had been stolen. The council, acknowledging the owners' claim to the right of possession, ordered that the Indians be delivered to Colonel James Moore "for the use and on behalf of the owners."

A case in Massachusetts shows a colonial government remunerating a citizen for an Indian slave taken from him by governmental authority. During King Philip's War, one George Speere bought an Indian from Captain Hull who had been empowered by the council to make sale of Indian captives at that time. The council, by warrant of the constable of Braintree, took away the Indian boy for some reason. Speere complained of the loss of his property, after, as he said, he had brought it to a "very tractable and profitable state" and petitioned to have his Indian boy returned to him, or to be given his value. The council accordingly granted him the value.

As in the case of other property, the colonial courts were sometimes called upon to settle disputes regarding the ownership of Indian slaves. Two events in Massachusetts and North Carolina are cases in point. In 1684, the Massachusetts Court of Assistants was called upon to settle a case of disputed ownership which had been appealed from the County Court of Salem. On November 24, 1777, complaint was made to the North Carolina House of Commons by a slave owner who had been dispossessed of his Indian slave by two other Carolinians. The House appointed a committee to investigate the matter. Similar instances in other years are recorded in connection with North Carolina.

With the growth of the idea of property incident to the slavery status, the early transition of the slave from personal estate to a chattel real, or real estate with accompanying incidents, was easy and natural.

Under the caption of property both negro and Indian slaves were subject to taxation like other property, either for colonial revenue in general or to meet local expenses. Moreover in certain colonies both Indian and negro slaves were assigned the double character of persons subject to a poll tax and property subject to a property tax.

South Carolina, in the act of 1690, provided "that all slaves . . . as to the payment of debts shall be deemed and taken as all other goods and chattels, . . . and all negroes and slaves shall be accounted as freehold in all other cases whatsoever and descend accordingly." Middleton, president of the council, consequently declared, in 1725, that negroes were real property, such as houses and lands, in Carolina. Yet they were always returned as personal property in the inventories of intestates. This condition continued until 1740, when it was declared that negroes and Indian slaves should be reputed and adjudged in law to be chattels personal in the hands of their owners and possessors and their executors, administrators and assigns. Various tax acts were passed from time to time for special reasons, and in some of these Indian slaves, along with negroes, were a part of the basis of taxation, being rated as property without specification as to real or personal, along with goods, lands, cattle and white servants. Such an act was passed in 1703. The act contained the general term "slaves," which, of course, included Indian slaves by implication.

A tax on polls was generally selected by the colonies as the chief source of revenue. In accordance with this idea of taxation North Carolina during the eighteenth century regarded Indian slaves as taxables. In the earliest legislative action of the colony taxables were declared to be every white male aged sixteen years, and every slave, negro, mulatto, or Indian, male or female, aged twelve years. By the act of 1750, furthermore, a taxable was every white man of sixteen years of age, every negro, mulatto or mustee, and every other person of mixed blood to the fourth generation, twelve years of age.

In Virginia, especially, there was much confusion regarding the position of the slave as a person and as property. Until after the Revolution, taxes were chiefly imposed according to the number of tithables in each county, i.e., persons assessed for a poll tax. The act of 1649 declared all imported male servants to be tithables. Indians, imported into the colony as servants were included by implication.

Since in the preceding year an act had declared that a specified poll tax should be levied only on the tithables, Indian servants, as they must be called before 1670, were attributed a legal personality or a membership in the social status inconsistent with the condition of a chattel or property. By the act of March, 1658, Indian servants, male and female, sixteen years of age, were included among the tithables by specific mention. The same provision was repeated in the acts of March, 1662. Some doubt having arisen as to whether this law applied to female Indian servants as well as to male, acts were passed in December, 1662, September, 1672 and November, 1682, to settle the matter. The former act related to women servants commonly employed in "working in the crop"; the latter declared that "all Indian women are and shall be tithables, and ought to pay levies in like manner as negro women brought into this country do, and ought to pay." In 1682, the gradual process of change from the status of Indian servitude to that of Indian slavery was completed. The Virginia act of 1670 had decreed a condition of slavery for all Indians imported into the colony by sea. But the great body of subject Indians were natives of the country. Such Indians remained servants up to 1676, when at the beginning of the Indian war, one of Bacon's laws made all Indian captives slaves.

In 1682, slavery was extended to captives sold by tributary Indians "in the hope of mitigating their condition as it was certain that they would be held in slavery by their captors. "These acts did not make provision for changing the condition of Indian servants that existed in the colony before 1670. Such a change had come about through a gradual and natural process with the passage of the laws mentioned and the changed attitude toward the subject Indians, so that in fact all subject Indians were not considered slaves. Hence, in 1682, all Indian slaves were considered in law as persons inasmuch as they were tithables. By 1705 it was found necessary, for legal purposes, to advance the property notion of the slave from personalty to realty, though certain incidents of personalty were still retained. The statute of that year by which the change was effected provided that in future "all negro, mulatto or Indian slaves in all courts of jurisdiction and other places within this dominion shall be held, taken and adjudged to be real estate and not chattels." As a part of real estate property slaves were subject to taxation. An act of 1748 again made slaves personal estate, but was repealed by the king, October 31, 1751. By the acts of 1779 and 1781 slaves were still liable to a poll tax of £5 and 10s. respectively, to be paid by the owner. So it may be seen that from 1649 until after the Revolution Indian servants and slaves either as persons or as property were used as a basis for taxation in Virginia.

Masachusetts was the only other colony that assigned the double status of personalty and real property to its slaves. There, as in Virginia, the status varied from time to time. Under the earliest laws of taxation in that colony, slaves must have been rated, if taxed at all, as polls, the owners paying for them as for other servants and children, "such as take not wages." This continued until 1692, when "every male slave of sixteen years old and upwards was rated at twenty pounds estate." But in 1694 "all negroes, mulattoes and Indian servants, as well male as female, of sixteen years old and upwards" were assigned a status of personalty by being rated at 12d. per poll, the same as other polls. In 1695, "all negro, mulatto and Indian servants" again became a property basis for taxation by an act valuing negro, mulatto and Indian male servants fourteen years of age and upward at £20 estate, and similar female servants at £14 estate, unless disabled by infirmity. They were subsequently, in 1696, rated as "other personal estate" which rating was continued in 1697 and 1698, in the latter year "according to the found judgment and discretion of the assessors, not excluding faculties", i.e., trades or professions. This rating for faculties was common throughout the early tax laws of Massachusetts, and continued into the nineteenth century. It was applied to white men from the beginning, but the law of 1698 appears to have been the first and only one in which the feature was applied to the negroes, mulattoes and Indians who were slaves. There was little variation in the tax laws during the remainder of the colonial period. All Indian, negro and mulatto servants continued to be rated as personal property in the usual yearly levies. Occasionally, as in the earlier period, some of those who were servants for a term of years, but not for life, were numbered and rated as polls. Other exemptions were made in the case of slaves "disabled by infirmity."

In 1716, an attempt was made to modify this feature of property status for slaves in Massachusetts. In that year Judge Sewall was a member of the council, and on June 22, 1716, proposed to that body that negro and Indian slaves be no longer rated with horses and hogs as personal property. The council agreed to the proposition, and its decision was sent down to the deputies for concurrence. But the members of the house refused assent on the ground that they were just going to make a new valuation. In the preceding valuations of the property of their constituents, Indian, negro and mulatto slaves were regarded as property, and the owners of it should be taxed accordingly.

In the remaining colonies that taxed Indian and other slaves, such taxation was levied on the basis of property, Sometimes personal and sometimes real. The annual tax in South Carolina included slaves among the taxable property. A law of 1719 provided that since Indian slaves were commonly reputed to be of less value than negro slaves, all persons possessing them should pay for each Indian in proportion to half the value of whatever might be rated and imposed for each negro, and no more.

In New York Indian and negro slaves entered but little into the system of taxation, since slaves were not numerous in the colony and therefore would furnish but a poor basis for taxation, and the finances of the colony were provided for more largely by income taxes than otherwise. In 1709, however, along with a tax on chimneys, fireplaces and stoves, a tax of two shillings was levied on every negro or Indian slave from fifteen to sixty years of age, with directions for collecting the same, and provision for fine and punishment if such tax were not paid. Again, in 1734, when arrangement was made to raise a certain amount yearly for a period of ten years, one source of revenue was to be a tax of "two pennyweight and twelve grains of Sivil Pillar or Mexican Plate, or the sum of one shilling in Bills of Credit made current in this colony" on every Indian or mulatto slave who was above the age of fourteen and under the age of fifty years.

An instance of Indian slaves serving as a basis of taxation in a local levy is found in the history of Rye, New York. At a town meeting in 1703, to raise the assessment for the ensuing year, it was decided that a portion of the sum should be obtained by the tax on £12 valuation of all slaves of sixteen years old and upward. Though Indian slaves were not mentioned in the town action, they were doubtless included by implication, for in 1711 the people of the town were called upon to pay taxes under "an act for raising one shilling on every Indian and negro slave."

In most of the colonies import duties, and in at least one instance export duties, were levied on Indian slaves brought into or taken from the colonies. Such duties were generally levied for self-defense, though occasionally for revenue. During the colonial period England's interest in the African slave trade led her to take effective measures to dispose of as many negroes as possible in the American colonies. In course of time the colonists awoke to the danger which might result from an excess of an ignorant Servile class which in some sections outnumbered the white population. Frequent attempts were made in various colonies to check the importation of negroes by levying import duties. At times Indians as well as negroes were included in these laws. In their enactment it seems probable that the colonial legislatures had a double purpose: to shut out undesirables of both races, and to prevent the importation of negroes in the guise of Indians. Real danger threatened the colonies from an excessive importation of Indians as slaves, and an attempt was therefore made to check it. In those colonies where import duties furnished a substantial part of the colonial revenue, such duties were levied on Indian slaves as well as on other property.

As early as 1698 the importation of negroes into South Carolina had reached such proportions that the safety of the province was considered endangered. Attempts to check such importation were accordingly made throughout the colonial period by levying import duties. As the number of Indian slaves in the colony increased, they too were included as a basis for duties. By the act of 1721, the importation of negro, mulatto, mustee and Indian slaves (Spanish Indians excepted) by their owners was permitted without duty, provided such owner intended to settle in the colony and employ the slaves in his own service. He was required, however, to take an oath that in case he sold any of these slaves within twelve months after bringing them into the colony, he would pay certain required duties.

The Spanish Indians were considered especially undesirable. Accordingly, an act of 1722 imposed upon all such Spanish Indians, negroes, mulattoes and mustees imported, a duty of £50 current money of the province. The duty on Indian slaves was levied without regard to age, while that on negro slaves was graduated according to age. A report to the Board of Trade, February 2, 1736, gave the duty on negro slaves imported from Africa above ten years old as £10; under ten years old, £5; and on all Indians imported, £50 each. The following was the tariff schedule on negroes and Indians in force in 1775. Indians imported as slaves, each £50. Negroes or slaves, four feet two inches or more in height, each £10. Negroes, under four feet two, and above three feet two inches, each £5. Negroes, under four feet two, and above three feet two inches, sucking children excepted, each £ 50. Negroes or slaves from any of his Majesty's plantations in America, where such slaves have been for six months or more, unless imported by the owners with design to be employed on their own account, besides the above £10, £5, and £2 10s., each slave, £50.

The earliest act passed in Virginia to check the importation of negroes, that of 1699, imposed a duty of fifteen shillings per poll upon every servant not born in England or Wales, and twenty shillings for every negro or other slave imported into the colony. This duty was continued or increased by a number of temporary acts between 1669 and 1776. The acts were worded "all slaves" or "negroes and other slaves." Thus import duties were levied upon Indian as well as negro slaves. A statute of 1710 advanced the duty on negroes to £5 per head, and placed a duty of twenty shillings on Indians imported by land. The difference in the amount of the duties is indicative of the relative amount of danger attached by the colonists to the presence of the two classes of slaves in the colony.

At the time of the Tuscarora War, the northern colonies realized fully the possible results of the importation of the captives sold in their communities. Some of them in consequence passed laws to ward off danger from this source. In 1712, Rhode Island passed an act levying a duty of forty shillings on every Indian brought into the colony. The act was enforced by severe penalties, and every ship owner was required to give bond to the amount of £50 for observing it. New Hampshire, in 1714, levied the heavy duty of £10 on the importation of any Indian into the province.

Pennsylvania, also, June 7, 1712, voted to levy a duty of £20 on all negroes and Indians brought into the colony by land or water, certain negroes from the West Indies excepted. Exception was also made in the case of negro and Indian slaves brought in by their owners with the intention of taking them out again within the space of twenty days, and in the case of Indians or negroes belonging to persons in the province and sent out of it on their masters' business with intent to return again.

A duty of £10 was levied by New Jersey in 1713. In January, 1739, the New Jersey assembly presented to the council for concurrence a bill entitled "An act for laying a duty on negro, Indian and mulatto slaves imported into this province." The bill did not appeal favorably to the council and was rejected. The reason for rejection was the need of laborers in the province, owing to the decrease in the number of white indentured servants, and the check that this bill would give to the importation of negroes. But in November, 1769, a bill setting forth as its purpose the encouragement of the coming of white servants by limiting the importation of blacks, was passed. The duty in this case was higher than that proposed in 1739, being £15 on all slaves imported, negro, Indian or mulatto. Punishment for refusal or neglect to pay was specified. Purchase of a slave "made upon the Water or Waters along the Seacoast" of the province, or on those between the province and the provinces of New York, Pennsylvania and the Lower Counties of the Delaware, was, by section VII of the act, declared a "purchase within the county" of New Jersey "opposite to such Water" and so was exempt from duty.

The second cause for levying duties on Indians and other slaves was to obtain revenue. Virginia in its legislation on the subject had pretended at least that such was its purpose, and to carry out the pretense had devoted the amounts thus obtained to meeting colonial expenses. Other colonies sought directly for revenue. New York was a striking example of such colonies. Import duties formed a chief source of the colonial revenue, and slaves were enumerated among the other commodities. The act of May 1, 1702, the first specifically to mention Indian slaves, placed a duty of fifteen shillings on every negro or Indian slave imported into the colony directly from their place of residence, and thirty shillings upon every negro or Indian slave not so imported. The act which was to continue but two years was found to be "of great use in this colony" and was accordingly repeated on August 4, 1705, to continue seven years. On June 24, 1719, it was again repeated to remain in effect from July 1, 1720, to July 1, 1726. Still other acts imposing similar duties were passed as follows: in 1709, levying a duty of £3 on every negro imported into the colony not directly from Africa and £3 on every other slave or slaves not directly imported into the colony from Africa, the act to continue till May 1, 1711: on June 21, 1714, levying "a duty of ten ounces of good plate" to be paid by the master or commander of any vessel, or any other person importing slaves; and on September 1, 1716, levying a duty of "ten ounces of good plate" on each negro, Indian or mulatto slave imported into the colony from Africa in any vessel not wholly owned by the people of the colony, and a like duty on every negro, Indian or mulatto slave imported into the colony from any part of the West Indies or any of the neighboring colonies, negroes or other slaves going to and fro on their owners' business excepted. On October 16, 1718, furthermore, it was decreed that no greater duty was to be demanded on any slave brought into the colony directly from Africa by a ship of Great Britain, than was to be demanded from vessels wholly owned by inhabitants of the colony. In June 17, 1726, on every Indian, negro or mulatto slave (male or female) of four years of age or upwards imported by land or water from all places other than Africa, a duty of £4 was laid. On October 14, 1732, a similar duty, regardless of the place from which the slave was imported, was laid. On November 28, 1734, on every negro, Indian or mulatto slave above the age of fourteen and under the age of fifty, during the period of ten years, the duty was fixed at "the quantity of two pennyweight and twelve grains of Sivil pillar or Mexican plate, or the sum of one shilling in Bills of Credit made current in this colony." On December 16, 1737, finally, every negro, Indian or mulatto slave above the age of four years imported directly from Africa was made dutiable at the rate of five ounces of "Sivil pillar or Mexican plate" or forty shillings in bills of credit current in the colony; and for every such slave imported from all other places by land or water, the sum of £4 in like money was exacted. All slaves belonging to the crew of any vessel, and slaves coming into the colony from the neighboring colonies upon the service of their masters, and all slaves under fourteen years of age were to be admitted free of duty.

Any person coming into the colony alone, or with his or her family to reside or visit in the colony, was allowed to bring slaves for personal service, provided the owner gave sufficient security to the treasurer within four days after the importation thereof, that, whenever such slaves should be sold, the duty imposed by the act should be paid within two days after such sale. Upon failure to pay such duty, the owner or disposer of such slaves was to forfeit the sum of £10, the slave or slaves, nevertheless, to be subject to the duty in question. The duties provided for by the act were to remain in existence for the period of one year. At the expiration of the act it was continued for another year, with certain amendments which did not relate to slaves. At the expiration of the specified period it was again continued for another year or until the close of 1740, when it was again continued until December, 1741. Such acts were then passed by New York each year until the opening of the troubles of the Revolutionary period.

The number of Indians exported as slaves from South Carolina was larger than that from any other colony. As a means of obtaining revenue, as well as of attempting to check the business of the Indian traders, the colony passed an act in 1703 which placed a duty upon Indian slaves ex ported from the colony. The traders were carefully instructed not to attempt any such exportations without first paying at Charleston the required duties, twenty shillings for each Indian exported.

CHAPTER X. METHODS OF EMPLOYMENT

SINCE the English never made long journeys of exploration into the interior, as the Spanish and French did in the earliest days of their occupation of America, their use of Indian slaves as hunters, fishermen and guides was relatively limited. With the forming of settlements and the growth of institutional life this use became more prominent. In Carolina it appears that the Indian slaves were occupied chiefly in hunting and fishing for their masters, whereas the greater part of the harder field work was left to the negroes. The Indians were expert hunters, and as the woods abounded in game, such a hunter "was of great service in a plantation, and could furnish a family with more provisions than they could consume." In New England, also, there is occasional mention of Indian slaves used as guides. It seems probable, however, that this service was more largely confined to the south where Indian slaves were less expensive and more easily procured than in the north, for such an occupation offered more opportunity for escape than any other.

In New England the Indians retained in the colonies as slaves after the Pequot and King Philip Wars were chiefly women and children. In the early history of Massachusetts some of the leading families in wealth and importance unable to obtain other help, employed Indians as cooks. After the wars in question the Indian slaves were put to the same use by both Massachusetts and Connecticut.

The colonial newspapers of New England attribute much domestic ability to the Indian slaves advertised in their columns: "An Indian woman who is a very good cook, and can wash, iron and sew"; "A likely Indian wench about nineteen years of age fit for any business in town or country"; "An Indian woman . . . fit for all manner of household work either in town or country, can sew, wash, brew, bake, spin and milk cows"; "A lusty Carolina Indian woman fit for any daily service." The newspapers of the middle colonies furnish a similar record: "A young Spanish Indian woman, fit for all manner of household business"; "An Indian woman and her child . . . she washes, irons and starches very well, and is a good cook."

The agricultural system of New England was not favorable to the use of slaves in the fields, yet there are occasional glimpses of Indian slaves employed in agricultural pursuits. In the account book of Lieutenant Stephen Longfellow, 1710, appears the item: "Bouston one day to plant". Bouston was his Indian slave. It has been considered probable, judging from the number of negro and Indian slaves in Rhode Island, that both were an important factor in developing the stock farming of the colony. The newspaper advertisements of the day offer some information on this point: "A Carolina Indian man fit for any service within doors or without"; "An Indian boy about sixteen years old, fit for either sea or land service"; "An Indian man . . . fit for any service"; "A Survanam Indian man, twenty-five years of age, who has been in the country thirteen years, fit for service in either country or town, and who can mow well."

In all the southern colonies Indian slaves worked in the fields side by side with the negroes up to the time of the Revolution. The discovery, about 1693, of rice as a profitable staple for export, made necessary a large supply of labor in South Carolina; hence along with the negroes so largely imported to meet the demand, the Indian slaves worked also as the plantation system grew. In South Carolina, Governor Moore employed some of his Indian slaves in tilling his fields.

The instances of Indian slaves employed by their owners in manual occupations are more numerous in New England than elsewhere. The newspapers furnish instances like the following: "An Indian lad about eighteen years old, a cooper by trade . . . can do anything at the carpenter's trade"; "An Indian lad . . . he can work at the weaver's trade." Similar advertisements are found in the New York papers: "An Indian man . . . a good carpenter, wheelwright, cooper and butcher."

Such instances are to be found even in the south. The training of Indian slaves to skilled labor was not generally considered politic, however, since it interfered with the coming to the colonies of white craftsmen who were so much desired. In 1743 or 1744, a committee in South Carolina, appointed to consider the most effectual means of increasing immigration to the province, included in the bill which it originated, a clause prohibiting the bringing up of negroes and other slaves to those mechanical trades in which white persons are usually employed.

Indian slaves were made a source of income to their owners by hiring them out to work in the same way as negroes and indentured white servants. The colonial laws in some instances made provision for such use. A South Carolina law of 1712 permitted an owner to hire out his slaves by the year or for a shorter time, and receive their earnings. The provision was repeated in acts of 1735 and 1740. Maryland, in 1753, provided that masters of ships might hire servants or slaves from their owners. New York City, in 1731, made provision for owners hiring out negro and Indian slaves. Since the custom was common in its application to other servile classes, one may believe that it was followed in other colonies besides those which made legal provision regarding it.

The use of Indian slaves in military operations was not infrequent. In the New England wars Captain Church employed Indian captives against the enemy, a plan which he found serviceable on several occasions. This use of Indian as well as negro slaves for military purposes was advocated in 1666 in a narrative addressed to the Duke of Albemarle.

In the intercolonial wars both negro and Indian slaves were captured by the French from the English army. In French records dealing with occurrences in Canada, under date of November 11, 1747, "four negroes and a Panis who were captured from the English during the war" are mentioned. Still another possible proof of the use of Indian slaves by the English army is found in the Articles of Peace drawn up at Niagara, July 18, 1764. They contain the following: "Article 2nd. That any English who may be prisoners or deserters, and any negroes, Panis, or other slaves who are British property, shall be delivered up within a month to the commandant of Detroit, and that the Hurons use all possible endeavors to get those who are in the hands of the neighboring nations, engaging never to entertain any deserters, fugitives or slaves, but should any fly to them for protection, they are to deliver them up to the next commanding officer."

That such slaves were put to practical use in the military preparations of the colonies, is seen in the New York City ordinances of 1693 and 1694 which provided that all persons, and all negro and Indian slaves that were not listed, should work on the fortifications.

Such a town action was not unusual. In 1638, the townsmen of Hartford, Connecticut, voted to levy on the cattle and slaves of the townspeople when needed for public service.

South Carolina on different occasions offered inducements for slaves to serve in the war. Some of these acts mentioned Indian slaves. In 1704, an act was passed "for raising and enlisting such slaves as shall be thought serviceable to this province in time of alarms." It provided for making a list of all negro, mulatto and Indian slaves in the province fit for service. The masters of the slaves were to be notified of such listing and given a chance to show cause why it should not be done. In case the slaves were called upon for service, the master must furnish weapons according to specifications. If the slave were maimed or killed in the service, the owner should be compensated out of the public treasury.

To provide still further for the use of slaves in war, it was decreed by a South Carolina act of 1719 that the captains, lieutenants, and ensigns of the militia companies should form a list of negro, mulatto, mustee and Indian slaves from sixteen to sixty years of age fit for military service. Owners were given a chance to show why such slaves should not serve. These slaves when enlisted were to be armed and equipped by the captain of the division, or they might be armed by their owners, the latter to be compensated for loss or damage to their arms. A fine of £20 was fixed for neglect of any owner to send his slave in time of alarm to the usual place of rendezvous of the various divisions. Any officer neglecting to carry out the terms of the act was to be fined £5. A slave serving in war was to be allowed £10 reward if, on the testimony of a white person, he could prove that he had killed one of the enemy in time of invasion. The owner was to be indemnified from the public funds for a slave killed or wounded.

In 1778, when Washington proposed to enlist slaves in the battalions raised by the State of Rhode Island, the assembly voted that every able bodied negro, mulatto or Indian man slave in the state might enlist in either battalion to serve during the continuance of the war. Such slave was to receive all the bounties, wages and encouragements allowed by the Continental Congress to any soldier enlisting in the service, and in addition was immediately to be set free.

It is noticeable that in this legislation regarding the use of slaves in war, no provision was made for their military training. Such training would require too much time, and besides being a loss to the owners, might prove dangerous to the colony if the slaves were sufficiently numerous. Maryland recognized this fact and in 1715 voted to exclude slaves from such training.

Just as the Spanish and the French made diplomatic and military use of their Indian slaves by returning them to their own tribes and thus winning friendship and peace, so the English followed the same practice. In 1715, in order to secure the aid of the Tuscarora, the assembly of South Carolina voted that, for every one of these allies killed in actual warfare by the enemy, a Tuscarora slave then in servitude among the whites should be given them for the loss, and that to every Tuscarora taking an Indian enemy captive, a slave of his nation should similarly be assigned as a reward.

CHAPTER XI. TREATMENT

THE treatment of Indian slaves apparently differed in no essential degree from that of the negroes. The slaves of the two races lived and worked together; but since the negroes were in the majority, the treatment of slaves in general was determined by the ordinary usage which the whites accorded them in particular. It is customary for writers dealing with early slavery among both the English and French of America to declare it mild in nature. The statement appears to be true. The system was patriarchal in nature, though it is doubtful if race feeling among the English was ever so nearly obliterated, and a condition of fellowship approaching equality ever so fully developed, as in the case of the French. Individual cases of cruelty and harsh treatment undoubtedly existed as they must exist in all cases of servitude; but Indian slavery never became an institution sufficiently well organized to make harsh treatment general. There was never anything in either the English or French colonies corresponding to the labor gang used by the Spanish. The number of Indian slaves in a locality was too small for that; nor did the service which the colonists required of their Indian slaves demand it. Kind treatment, however, did not exclude the infliction of corporal punishment, if thought needful.

To judge from the frequent newspaper advertisements of runaways, the Indian slaves of the English colonists were at least comfortably dressed. The following are typical extracts from the newspapers of the various colonies: "a black crape gown and a striped stuff jacket"; "a blue flannel petticoat, a dark Estamine gown and a double striped gown"; "a grey coat with pewter buttons, with leather breeches, an old tow shirt, grey stockings, good shoes and felt hat"; "a green hat and yellow breeches"; "an orange colored broadcloth coat, with a narrow cape, and a flannel jacket with narrow stripes, a cotton shirt, and a loose pair of Oxenbridge trousers . . . a beaver hat, and had a bundle of clothes with him"; "an old blue coat, striped flannel jacket, pretty good hat, black wig, linen trousers, white yarn stockings, and an old pair of mended shoes"; "a good felt hat, orange colored jacket, thick leather breeches, checked wool shirt, light grey stockings and pretty good shoes"; "pea-jacket of light brown, leather breeches, shoes, stockings and hat"; "a drugat waistcoat and kersey petticoat of a light color." From these advertisements it appears that the slaves were dressed much like the colonists themselves, though doubtless their clothing often consisted of "cast offs." In the Carolinas where slaves were more numerous, coarse goods were-imported by the planters for slaves' clothing. Mention is found of "serge suits for the servant maids, of coarse kerseys, tufted holland jackets, etc." with which the plantation was wont to be supplied for the slaves and convict servants. These were used in addition to cloth woven and made into clothes by the women of the household.

Generally kind as the treatment of Indian slaves may have been, the sentiment of the English colonists was quite opposed to the intermingling of whites and Indians, bond or free, even if in the early history of Virginia there was some effort made to encourage the marriage of whites and free Indians. It was natural, therefore, that definite action should be taken to prevent the marriage of free whites and Indian slaves. In 1691, Virginia passed an act forbidding the union of free whites with Indians whether slave or free; but there seems to have been no provision against marriage of negroes or Indians with white indentured servants. The provision, perhaps, was unnecessary, for the consent of the white indentured servant's master was necessary for the validity of such a union, and such consent was usually refused because of the strong prejudice against race mixture.

North Carolina, also, in 1715, passed an act forbidding the marriage of whites with negroes, mulattoes or Indians, under penalty of £50, and making clergymen celebrating such a marriage liable to a fine of £50. A later act of 1741 provided a fine of £50 for the marriage of any white man or woman with an Indian, negro, mustee, mulatto, or any person of mixed blood to the third generation, bond or free. Any minister or justice of the peace performing such a Service was punishable by a fine of £50. Maryland, on its own part, in 1692, passed an act against the marriage or promiscuous sexual relations of whites and negroes or other slaves. Any white person so offending was to become a servant for seven years, if free at the time of the marriage. If already a servant, he or she must serve seven years after the end of the present term of service.

The same feeling existed in New England. A Massachusetts act of 1692 forbade the marriage, under severe penalty, of any white person with a negro, Indian or mulatto. Mixed marriages of whites and Indians, like those admired by Sewall in 1702, did occur, however, in New England, and it appears probable that some of these marriages were with the enslaved captives of King Philip's War and the Indian slaves imported from Carolina.

Considering, further, the determination of legal relations between the whites and the Indian slaves, it should be remembered that, when not specifically referred to, Indian slaves were included by implication in the legislative acts of the various colonies relating to slaves. Sufficient proof of this statement lies in the fact that Indian slaves are directly mentioned in certain of the legislative acts of any given colony, whereas other acts of the same colony specify slaves, negroes and other slaves, or negro and mulatto slaves. In one colony, Virginia, the term "mulatto" was made to include Indians by the act of 1705, which provided that the child of an Indian should be "deemed, accounted, held and taken to be a mulatto."

It was a part of the universal law of slavery in the southern colonies that a slave should not be allowed to testify against a white person in the courts. South Carolina, by the acts of 1712, 1722 and 1735, permitted "negroes and other slaves" to testify in the trial of any slave accused of specified crimes and offenses. Certain of the colonies, by express provision, forbade Indian slaves to give testimony in the trial of whites. North Carolina declared that "all negroes, mulattoes, bond and free to the third generation, and Indian servants and slaves, shall be deemed to be taken as persons incapable in law to be witnesses in any case whatever except against each other." Virginia, 1705, decreed that "popish recusants, convict negroes, mulattoes and Indian servants and others not being Christians, shall be deemed and taken to be persons incapable in law to be witnesses in any case whatsoever." In 1732, the same colony decreed that the evidence of any negro or Indian slave might be received in the trial of any slave, but was not valid in the trial of any other person. Maryland declared, in 1717, that it would be dangerous to allow the evidence of any negro, mulatto or Indian slave in the trial of a freeman, but conceded that, if evidence was lacking in cases regarding any negro, mulatto or Indian slaves, that such slaves might give testimony for or against themselves and one another. In some of the northern colonies, at least, acts were passed forbidding slaves to give testimony in the trial of white persons. The New York law of 1706 is a case in point. This feature of the law of evidence was renewed from time to time in the various colonies and continued until the Revolution.

The right to life was generally conceded all slaves regardless of color. At least one colony, New Hampshire, 1708, in an act guaranteeing this right, included Indian slaves by specific mention. This and other rights could be protected by appeal to the courts. If not otherwise provided for, the mode of trial used by the colonists themselves was employed in the case of Indian slaves, negroes and free Indians. Special legislation concerning the trial of slaves was enacted by all the English colonies. It has been said that for an Indian to gain his point in an English court, unless his case was an extremely strong one, was a rare occurrence. Whether the statement is generally true in the case of either free or slave Indians, might be difficult to decide. Doubtless the Indian slave supported by his master possessed a better chance of obtaining justice than the free Indian. Since a slave was owned body and soul, and therefore had no right to life except as the same might be conceded by his owner and the authorities, it may be said that whatever legal rights he had were granted for the protection of the slave owners in their property rights and for the general safety of the community, rather than because of any special consideration of justice toward the slave himself.

Virginia, in 1692, provided special courts for the trial of slaves. The provisions regarding these courts were changed from time to time. By the act of 1765 it was provided that the justices be given a standing commission of oyer and terminer empowering them to try without a jury all criminal offenses committed by slaves in their respective counties. In accordance with these provisions one finds the Earl of Dunmore issuing a commission in 1772 to certain justices in the county of the present state of West Virginia, authorizing them to serve as a court for the trial of negro and Indian slaves.

The Massachusetts general court provided, 1647, that one or more of the magistrates, according to agreement among themselves, should hold a court every quarter to hear and determine all cases civil and criminal, except those involving capital punishment, which might concern Indians, and that minor offenses should be tried by the sachems themselves. At the first general court held on Martha's Vineyard, June 18, 1672, it was ordered that an Indian should have liberty in any case to appeal from such courts as they held among themselves to the quarter court, and from the quarter court to the general court.

A New Jersey act of 1713 provided for the trial of any negro, Indian or mulatto slave accused of committing murder, rape, etc., by a justice and five freeholders. But if the owner of such slave should desire a jury, the privilege might be allowed him. He also had the right to challenge jurors as in other cases of like nature. The act was repealed in 1768.

By a New York act of 1712, three justices and five freeholders of the county constituted judge and jury, seven making a quorum, for the trial of negro and Indian slaves accused of murder, rape, insurrection or conspiracy. The prosecution provided the accusation to which the offended was obliged to plead apparently without the aid of counsel. The owner of the slave was given the right, however, to have his slave tried by a jury of twelve, provided he paid the jury charges of nine shillings. An act of 1730 changed the required number of justices to three, one to be a quorum, associated with five of the principal freeholders of the county. Agreement of seven was required for the decision. In this case, as before, the owner could have his slave tried by a jury of twelve if he paid the jury charges of nine shillings.

There was a general tendency among slave owners to conceal crimes committed by slaves, or to secrete slave offenders and thus avoid the financial loss consequent upon the time consumed by the trial and the possible imprisonment of the slave in case of conviction, as well as the possible injury to the slave by corporal punishment, or the still greater loss of the slave's entire value in case of his execution. To prevent this interference with justice, as well as to recognize and protect the property rights of the slave owners, special acts were passed in some of the colonies providing that the slave owner be remunerated by the colonial government in case of the loss of his slave through execution for crime. In some colonies the amount to be paid the owner of a slave was specified by law, and this amount varied from £30 for a man slave, and £20 for a woman slave (negro, Indian or mulatto), as provided for in a New Jersey act of 1713, to £50 in a South Carolina act of 1717. In other colonies the amount to be paid the slave owner was left to the decision of the court. The Maryland act of 1717 is a case in point. It provided that the court should value the slave (negro, mulatto or Indian) in tobacco, and that three-fourths of the value thus adjudged should be allowed in the public levy to be paid to the owner of the slave.

In all of the colonies the conduct of Indian slaves as well as that of other slaves was necessarily subject to police regulations, and punishments were decreed for their violation. These regulations did not differ greatly in the various colonies, for the problems arising from the use of slaves varied but little in their nature. Among the prohibitions laid on Indian slaves specifically were the following: to be away from home without the owner's permission; the possession of fire arms; and engaging in certain kinds of traffic. Boston decreed, 1728, that no Indian, negro or mulatto should carry stick or cane within the town. In 1778, when forming its first proposed constitution, Massachusetts excepted from the franchise "negroes, Indians and mulattoes, bound and free." In an act of 1660 the Connecticut general court declared that neither negro nor Indian servants should be required to "train, watch or ward." In 1676, New York City excluded all Indian and negro slaves from the privilege of being carters, and in the same year passed an act to prevent the revels of Indian and negro slaves at inns. An ordinance of the Albany city council, 1686, forbade any negro or Indian slave to drive a cart within the city. A New York act of 1731, also, provided for regulating the conduct of negroes and Indians in the night time.

Few of the acts of colonial legislatures decreeing punishment for various offenses mention Indian slaves; yet in the following colonies the death penalty was to be inflicted upon Indian slaves convicted of certain crimes: by North Carolina, in 1741, for the second offense of killing horses, cattle or hogs, and for stealing, mismarking or misbranding such animals; by New Jersey, in 1713, for murder, or conspiracy, or attempt to murder, and in 1768, for rape, for wilfully burning any dwelling-house, barn, stable, outhouse, stacks of corn or hay, for wilfully mutilating, maiming or dismembering any person, for manslaughter, for stealing any sum of money above the value of £5, and for committing any felony or burglary.

Branding as a punishments for Indian slaves was decreed by the Massachusetts general court. Runaway Pequot slaves were so punished. Judging from the descriptions of runaway Indian slaves contained in the colonial newspapers, some form of branding or marking such culprits was used until a late period. These brands or marks sometimes took the form of letters or symbols pricked into the skin by gunpowder or India ink. They were placed usually on the forehead or the cheeks.

Whipping, the most common punishment provided by law for Indian as well as other slaves, was decreed by different colonies as follows: by North Carolina, in 1741, to consist of thirty-nine lashes well laid on, for giving false testimony in court, killing any domestic animal without the owner's consent, and for stealing, mismarking or misbranding such animals; by Pennsylvania, in 1721, for making, selling or using any fireworks or firearms in Philadelphia, and in 1751, for taking part in horse races or shooting matches without a license, fifteen lashes for the first offense and twenty-one for the second; by New Jersey, in 1713, for stealing to the value of six pence; by New York City, in 1682, for absence from their owners' homes or plantations without ticket of leave in owners' handwriting, in 1683, ten lashes for meeting together at any place on Sunday or any other day in groups of more than four, and possessing arms, unless the owner paid six shillings in lieu of the penalty, in 1713 and 1731, thirtynine lashes for being found in the city streets, if above the age of fourteen years, later than one hour after sunset, in 1721, and 1731, for gambling, in 1731, for attending a funeral in groups of more than twelve, for disorderly riding through the streets, and for selling "the Fish Commonly Called and known by the name of Bass" in the months of December, January and February, and in 1759, for committing any nuisance in the streets; by Connecticut, in 1750, forty lashes for publishing or speaking such words of and concerning any other person, which, if spoken or published by a white person, would be considered by law objectionable, and for being abroad after nine o'clock at night; and by Massachusetts, in 1693, for dealing in stolen goods. The town of Medford, Massachusetts, ordered, in 1734, that all negro, Indian or mulatto slaves found abroad without leave and not on their masters' business were to be punished by whipping. Block Island, finally, in 1709, provided ten lashes as punishment for any negro or Indian slave abroad after nine o'clock at night.

Punishment by mutilation was sometimes used, especially in the southern colonies. North Carolina, in 1741, provided that any slave, negro or Indian, giving false testimony in any court was to have an ear nailed to the pillory and to stand there for an hour, after which the ear was to be cut off. The other ear was then to be nailed in like manner and cut off at the expiration of an hour. By the same act the cutting off of both ears was made a partial punishment for killing horses, cattle or hogs without the consent of the owner, and for stealing, misbranding or mismarking such animals.

Certain of the colonies attempted to prevent the sale of spirituous liquors to Indian and other slaves. At the time of King Philip's War, Massachusetts forbade the sale of liquor without license to any Indian or negro. New Hampshire, 1686, passed a similar act. In the same year the common council of Albany prohibited the selling of liquor to Indian slaves without the owners' permission.

Considering still another phase of treatment, namely, that which had to do with religious instruction, it may be said that, among the early regulations of the British government for the colonies, it was required that measures be taken whereby "slaves may be best invited to the Christian faith and be made capable of being baptized therein." In the instructions to the colonial governors the home government not infrequently gave directions for the conversion of both negroes and Indians, but the Indians referred to were free, not slave. The enslaved natives were in too great a minority to attract attention; but any effort to instruct and convert the negroes must, of course, include the former by implication.

The good intentions of the home government for the conversion of slaves were commonly frustrated by the popular belief that baptism conferred freedom upon slaves. The general attitude of slave owners in all the colonies was to oppose or forbid the religious instruction and conversion of negro and Indian slaves. They argued that the instruction and conversion of slaves tended to make them disrespectful and unreliable and hence decreased their value.

Consequently the religious training of slaves in the earlier colonial period depended upon the personal teaching of the owner's family. This conditions of affairs appealed strongly to the missionaries of the Society for the Propagation of the Gospel in Foreign Parts on their coming to America primarily to work among the Indian tribes. In the reports sent to their Society early in the eighteenth century they lamented the unenlightened condition of the slaves, and urged that they be allowed to work among them where they believed their efforts would accomplish more than among the Indian tribes. The Society granted their requests and gave them special instructions to look after the spiritual interests of all slaves. Their subsequent reports, though they dealt primarily with negro slaves, sometimes made mention of Indian slaves, and show that there was no distinction in religious matters between the slaves of the two races.

A letter from Samuel Thomas to the Society, December 21, 1705, told of the employment of negro and Indian slaves on the Lord's Day; but in a memorial of the same year he rejoiced in the prospect of bringing many Indian and negro slaves to the knowledge and practice of Christianity. In a letter of the following year he urged that the Society give the missionaries strict charge to labor with great diligence in the conversion of the Indian and negro slaves in the respective parishes. In 1710, he reported that there was several unconverted Apalachee slaves in his parish whom he was especially anxious to baptize. Le Jau, another missionary in South Carolina, reported, in 1708, that the masters opposed the baptism and marriage of their slaves, and declared that "many masters cannot be persuaded that negroes and Indians are otherwise than beasts and use them like such." In the same year he reported many Indian and negro slaves instructed and on probation for baptism.

In 1710, also, certain masters had so far yielded in their opposition to the religious training of slaves as to allow Indian and negro slaves to remain a half-hour after the Services for instruction. In 1711, one Indian slave and thirty negro slaves had joined the church in his parish, and he was catechizing "negroes and other slaves" with their masters' consent, though then, and even at a later period, other masters in the same parish (Goose Creek) opposed his work among the slaves. Where such consent was granted, the slaves were often required to declare that they were not being baptized out of any effort to free themselves. From still another South Carolina parish (St. Thomas) the pastor, Haskell, wrote in 1711 that he was encouraging the conversion of Indian and negro slaves, and that he was also trying to persuade their masters to his mind. He met with some success, for another letter of the same year recorded the baptism of two negroes and an Indian slave. As late as 1730, however, he reported that the religious instruction of Indian and negro slaves was obstructed by irreligious and worldly people. In 1707, Dunn, the pastor of a parish thirty miles from Charleston reported that he met great difficulty in persuading masters to allow their Indian and negro slaves to receive religious instruction or to be baptized, since they believed that baptism would free slaves.

The same attitude of masters concerning the religious instruction of their slaves was reported from other colonies by the missionaries of the Society in question. But since the number of Indian slaves in no other colony was as large as in South Carolina, the mention of them by the missionaries is far less frequent, when made at all. Sharpe of New York, in a letter of 1712, mentioned two Spanish Indian slaves who were Christians. Neau of New York reported much opposition of masters to his work among the slaves. But Governor Cornbury promised to help him, and evidently his labors were successful, for a report in 1726 alluded to fourteen hundred negro and Indian slaves, many of whom had been instructed by Neau.

Since in general the religious instruction of servants and slaves was recognized as a duty by both the civil and ecclesiastical authorities in England, the response of the Society for the Propagation of the Gospel in Foreign Parts to these letters and reports was encouraging, and the missionaries were directed to do all in their power for the education and conversion of all slaves. On one occasion the Society went so far as to draft a bill to be introduced into Parliament providing for the more effectual conversion of negroes and servants in the plantation, and also petitioned the Archbishop of Canterbury that his majesty be requested to encourage the passage of laws in the colonies to the effect that baptism did not confer freedom upon slaves.

The colonial clergy similarly tried to obtain legislation at home which might serve to dispel the popular illusion that baptism conferred freedom upon slaves. A proposition contained in Mr. Forbes' account of the state of the church in Virginia, July 21, 1724, is a case in point. It stated that the Christian duty of instructing and educating heathen slaves in the Christian faith was much neglected by slave owners in America, though recommended by his majesty's instructions. It was accordingly proposed that every Indian, negro or mulatto child that should be baptized and publicly catechized by the minister in church, and who could, before the fourteenth year of his or her age, give a distinct account of the creed, the Lord's Prayer and the ten commandments, should, if the owner received a certificate from the minister to that effect, be exempted from paying all levies till the age of eighteen years.

Laws to this effect were passed in some of the colonies. The Carolina Fundamental Constitutions of 1669 had provided that it should be lawful for slaves to become members of any church or religious profession as if they were freemen, but that every owner should have absolute power and authority over his slaves regardless of their opinion or religion. But by the so-called "Church Act" of 1706, South Carolina showed itself averse to the policy advocated in the Constitutions of 1669, and decreed that the register of a parish should except negro and Indian slaves from the entries of births, christenings, marriages and burials. The law suited the times and was accordingly followed. But in 1712, in order to correct the popular misconception that a Christianized slave was by law free, an act was passed to the effect that baptism of slaves did not confer freedom upon them.

As early as 1655, the Virginia assembly had voted that Indian servants should be educated and brought up in the Christian faith. Yet the idea that baptism conferred freedom upon a slave even then existed in the colony, since one of the reasons given for the disallowance of the sale of an Indian boy by "The Kinge of Waineoke" to Elizabeth Short in 1659 was that the boy was desirous of baptism. The above action of the legislature probably contributed to the enactment of the law of 1667 which decreed that the baptism of a slave did not confer freedom upon him or in any way change his condition. The act naively declared the reason for this legislative action to be that masters freed from this doubt might the more carefully encourage the propagation of Christianity by permitting the conversion of slaves. The act of 1670, when slaves were for the first time legally designated as such in Virginia, decreed that freedom resulting from Christianity was limited to servants imported by shipping. Consequently Indian servants or slaves, since they generally came into the colony by land, were not eligible to become freemen by the provision. The act of 1670 was repealed in 1682 and a new act removed the possibility of conversion to Christianity conferring freedom upon any slaves, negro, mulatto or Indian, by decreeing that whether converted to Christianity before or after being brought to the colony, they should remain slaves. Finally, in 1712, Virginia passed a law requiring that the parents of free-born children and the owners of slave-born children, within twenty days after the birth of a child, should give notice in writing of the birth, with name and sex, the names of the parents of a free-born child, and the name of the owner of a slave-born child. The death of a slave was to be reported to the minister of the parish in the same way, and the minister was required to keep a record of all births and deaths in his parish. Virginia parish registers after this date contain records of the death of Indian slaves. Maryland, also, by the acts of 1692, 1694, 1704 and 1715 sought to encourage the baptism of "negroes and other slaves" by asserting that baptism did not confer freedom upon slaves or their offspring. In accordance with the instructions of Queen Anne to Governor Cornbury, 1702, New Jersey passed an act in May, 1704, declaring that baptism of any negro, Indian or mulatto slave should not be considered reason or cause for his freedom.

The amended "Duke's Laws" published about 1674, decreed that turning Christian should not set at liberty any negro or Indian servant in New York who had been bought by any person. Evidently the colonists put but little faith in this provision, for Governor Dongan reported in 1687 that they "take no care of the conversion of their slaves." The old idea that conversion conferred freedom upon slaves prevailed, and was doubtless strengthened by an order of the council, October 11, 1687, that Christian Indians and children of Christian parents brought from Campeachy and Vera Cruz as slaves should be set free, and by a similar order in the following year that Spanish Indian slaves professing Christianity were to be released and sent home. This last order was accompanied by a decree of the council, July 30, 1688, that the Spanish Indian slaves of certain persons be brought before it with a view of liberating them if they were able to say the Lord's Prayer. A report of Governor Bellomont, April 27, 1699, also, states that a "Bill for facilitating the conversion of negroes and Indians . . . would not go down with the assembly; they having a notion that the negroes being converted to Christianity would emancipate them from their slavery, and loose them from their service." But an act of October 24, 1706, "to encourage the Baptizing of Negro, Indian and Mulatto slaves" stated that the baptism of slaves did not confer freedom upon them. This partially calmed the fears of the slave owners, and the baptism of slaves became more frequent; but it did not lead the owners in all cases to favor the work of the missionaries among the slaves. In 1724, Mr. Jenney reported to the Society for the Propagation of the Gospel in Foreign Parts: "There are a few negroes and Indian slaves . . . in my parish: the catechist, a school-master from the honorable society, has often proposed to teach them the catechism, but we cannot prevail upon their masters to spare them from their labor for that good work." Again, in 1728, Mr. Wetmore reported the opposition of Quaker, Presbyterian and Episcopalian masters to the instruction and baptism of their slaves, but in 1734 he alluded to the baptism of one adult Indian slave.

In New England the earliest action taken by the colonial government with regard to the religious instruction of slaves occurred in 1677 in connection with the disposal as slaves of the captives taken in King Philip's War, when it was decreed that all the Indian slaves distributed among the inhabitants of the colony should "be taught and instructed in the Christian religion." How far such religious training was carried out would be difficult to ascertain. Occasional glimpses of the situation can be obtained. Experience Mayhew lamented that all the English did not instruct their servants in the "principles of the true religion"; though he cited instances when Indian servants, some of whom may have been slaves, were so instructed. Just how much missionary work was done in the homes of Massachusetts or elsewhere for the conversion of Indian servants and slaves is not known. Indian slaves were owned by ministers of the gospel, and it may be supposed that some attention was given to their instruction. Evidently the religious spirit of the Massachusetts colonists was sufficiently strong to include Indian slaves and servants, for in some churches negroes and Indians had a special location assigned them in the church and occasional reference is found to Indian slaves being church members. According to the baptismal records of November 19, 1727, for example, the Indian slave of Lieutenant Stephen Longfellow, great-great-grandfather of the poet, was his fellow member in the Byfield church. In this same year the Reverend Timothy Cutler reported from Boston: "Negro and Indian slaves belonging to my parish are about thirty-two, their education is according to the houses they belong to. I have baptized but two. But I know of the masters of some others who are disposed to this important good of their slaves and are preparing them for it; however, there is too great a remissness upon this article." In Rhode Island, also, for a long period the slaves were excluded from the church because their owners considered church membership to be inconsistent with their position. Finally in 1721 James MacSparran, pastor of Narragansett, protested against denying slaves the benefit of religious instruction and activities, and carried his point. After that date Indian and other slaves could belong to the churches, though baptism and membership were still held in disfavor by the slave owners. Connecticut, too, in 1727, favored the work of the church by enacting that masters and mistresses of Indian children were to use their utmost endeavors to instruct them in the Christian faith.

The popular idea that baptism conferred freedom upon slaves aroused eventually so much discussion among both the colonists and the representatives of the Society for the Propagation of the Gospel in Foreign Parts, and so many inquiries were addressed to the home government concerning the matter, that in 1729 the opinions of Talbot and Yorke, the attorney and solicitor generals of England, were expressed on the subject. Their decision was in accord with the acts of the various colonial legislatures to the effect that baptism did not confer freedom upon slaves. The declaration of Gibson, Bishop of London, about the same time, also, that "Christianity and the embracing of the Gospels does not make the least alteration in civil property" practically ended the discussion.

Turning now to a consideration of the question of manumission, it may be said that an Indian slave, like a negro of like condition, might obtain freedom during the latter's lifetime, or by testamentary disposition at the owner's death. His freedom might be purchased either by himself or others. A colonial court might declare him free if it were found that he was illegally held or misused. A colonial government, also, might grant him freedom for some special service rendered.

Action of the owner was naturally the most common way of conferring freedom. When freedom was bestowed during the owner's lifetime, a deed of manumission was usually given in order to avoid future complications. Occasionally in special instances the colonial government recognized such action of the slave owners as legal. For instance, the South Carolina Board of Counsel, August 3, 1711, in its directions to the Indian traders provided that any Indians taken captive in war and declared free by their respective masters who had a right so to act, should be deemed free men.

Record exists of Indian slaves purchasing their freedom from two sources, viz.: the colonial governments that held them before they were transferred to individual owners, and the individual masters themselves. In Plymouth, March 5, 1668, it was ordered that a certain Indian held at Boston "for matter of fact," since there was "a probability of a tender of some land for his ransom from being sent to Barbadoes" should be freed from such slavery on the tender of the land in question. A similar instance occurred in Connecticut. One of the earliest land grants of that colony was conveyed to its owner by the Indian chief, Uncas, in 1678, in exchange for Betty, an Indian woman taken captive in King Philip's War. Experience Mayhew relates the instance of an Indian slave who, after his master's death, purchased his freedom from his mistress on easy terms, "his master having never designed to keep him a slave all his days." Another instance, in 1709, shows an Indian slave woman sold to a free Indian to become his wife, in return for certain land.

By South Carolina law, an Indian slave was given a chance to prove his right to freedom. According to the act of 1712, any negro, mulatto, mustee or Indian slave, claiming freedom for certain reasons specified in the act, had the right to have his case heard and determined by governor and council. The act was repeated in 1722. By the terms of the acts of 1735 and 1740, and any slave might apply to the justices of the Court of Common Pleas by petition or motion. The court would then appoint a guardian for "said negro or Indian, mulatto or mestizo" and, after hearing evidence, would render decision. The alleged owner might defend himself, and if the plaintiff were declared free, the jury might award damages to the defendant. If the defendant should win the case, the court might inflict such corporal punishment on the plaintiff as it should see fit, not extending to danger to life or limb. The burden of proof was to lie with the plaintiff, and any such negro, Indian, etc., was to be considered a slave until the contrary was proved. Other courts of the province besides the one mentioned, were to have similar jurisdiction in the matter.

Certain of the colonies specified how slaves might be emancipated. In 1723, Virginia declared that no negro, mulatto or Indian slave was to be set free upon any pretense whatever except for some meritorious service, to be adjudged and allowed by the governor and council for the time being, and a license therefor first obtained. If any slave should be set free by his owner in any other way, it was declared lawful for the churchwardens of the parish wherein such slave should reside for the space of one month following his being freed, to take up and sell the said negro, mulatto or Indian as a slave at the next court held for the county. North Carolina, similarly, in 1741, provided that no slave was to be freed except for meritorious service, to be adjudged and allowed by license of the county court. If any owner should free his slave in any other way, the church wardens of the parish wherein such "negro, mulatto or Indian" should be found at the expiration of six months after the manumission, were authorized and required to sell the said negro, mulatto or Indian as a slave at the next session of the county court.

The colonial governments themselves granted freedom to Indian slaves on special occasions. By an act passed in 1660, Virginia provided that an Indian sold by another Indian, or an Indian who spoke the English language and who might desire baptism, should be given his or her freedom. In 1675, also, the Massachusetts general court freed the sister of an Indian whose friendship it wished to assure. The alleged owner of the slave being able to prove his title, the court ordered that £5 be paid for the slave's liberty.

At the time of King Philip's War the general courts of Massachusetts Bay and Plymouth reserved the privilege, not only of disposing of captives as slaves, but also of taking these slaves away from their owners and giving them their liberty if such action seemed advisable. In March, 1679, the Massachusetts general court made reparation in money to the master of an Indian slave, when for some reason the court freed the slave. The Plymouth general court, June 3, 1679, ordered the release of a certain Indian woman and her husband upon the payment by the woman's brothers of £6 in New England silver money. The same order provided in the case of a "younger Indian" that he should remain with his master until twenty-four years old, and then be given his freedom. Like action was taken in 1714 when the owner of an Indian slave petitioned the Massachusetts general court for the payment of £25, the prime cost which he paid for an Indian boy lately called out of his hands to be returned to the Indians at the time of the late pacification, besides charges in keeping and clothing of him and for doctors. Just prior to Church's expedition in King Philip's War, furthermore, as a military measure to prevent conspiracy among the Indians in the colony and their union with the warring tribes, Massachusetts decreed that any Indian servant discovering any dangerous plot or conspiracy of Indians should be emancipated, and his master be paid out of the public treasury a reasonable price for his services.

Some of the colonies considered it advisable to make regulations regarding the Indians after emancipation. A Virginia act of 1670 specified that former Indian slaves though baptized and enjoined their own freedom could not purchase Christian white servants. The law did not debar them, however, from buying any of their own race. Both New York by the act of 1712, and New Jersey by the act of 1713, decreed that no freed Indian could hold any real estate property in the colony concerned. South Carolina and North Carolina, also, regarded the presence of manumitted Indians in the colony as undesirable. The possibility that freedmen of this sort might stir up disturbance among their fellows who remained in slavery was too great a risk. A South

Carolina act of 1722 decreed that, if owners freed any slave, they must make provision for his passage out of the province. Such freedman, if he did not leave the province within twelve months after his manumission (being at liberty to do so) would lose the benefit of his emancipation, and continue to be a slave, unless the manumission were confirmed by both houses of the legislature. A further act of 1735 required that the slave when manumitted should quit the province within the period of six months following his manumission, and not return within seven years. The North Carolina act of 1741 specified that, if any freedman did not depart from the province within six months following his manumission, or should thereafter return to the province, the church wardens of the parish where he might be at the end of one month after his return, were to sell him at public auction at the next session of the county court.

The freeing of slaves who after their manumission might possess no means of support and in consequence become a burden upon the community, presented a problem that often needed attention. Connecticut understood the value of freeing worn-out slaves so as to avoid supporting them in their time of uselessness; hence in 1702 the general court enacted that every slave owner who freed his slave should in the years following manumission, if the former slave came to want, meet the expense which the local government encountered in caring for the freedman. The act was renewed by the court in 1703. Another act of practically the same tenor and including "Spanish Indians" was passed in 1711. An act of 1777, also, relieved the former owner of a freedman from any obligation to contribute to his support if the act of manumission had been sanctioned in due form by the selectmen of the former owner's town.

A New York law of 1712, on the other hand, provided that any one manumitting "any negro, Indian or mulatto slave" should give security of not less than £200 to pay yearly to such freed slave the sum of £20 lawful money of the colony. If the slave were freed by will and testament, the executors of the deceased person were required to give the same security after probate. If such security were not given, the manumission should be void. Since the law proved to be unsatisfactory, in 1717 it was amended so as to provide that any master or other person manumitting an Indian or negro slave should give security at the General Sessions of the Peace for city and county where such freed Indian or negro should reside, to keep such freedman from becoming a charge on the city, town or place.

New Jersey, too, in 1713, passed an act declaring that no negro or mulatto slave could be manumitted unless the slave's master gave surety to pay such freed slave £20 yearly. This is the only section of the act which did not include Indian slaves in its provisions. Evidently the omission was unsatisfactory, for a later act, November 16, 1769, repealed the section and provided that, if any owner should by will or otherwise free "any negro, Indian or mulatto slave" then such owner, his heirs or executors, at the next session of the Court of General Quarter Sessions of the Peace in the county where such owner resided, must give a bond of £200, so as to indemnify the community if such freedman became a pauper.

INDIAN SLAVERY

CHAPTER XII. THE DECLINE OF INDIAN SLAVERY

THE Small number of the Indians within the territory actually occupied by the English had its influence upon both the extent and the decline of Indian slavery. The Indians were never as numerous in the English territory as in that occupied or claimed by the Spanish and French. From many estimates made of the Indian population in the section under English rule, it would seem that the supply was sufficient to nourish the system of Indian slavery indefinitely; but it must be noted that the greater portion of this Indian population was made up of tribes generally remote from the English settlements.

The consensus of opinion to-day is that the number of Indians in New England about the year 1600 was not greater than twenty-four or twenty-five thousand. This number was so much reduced by the plague of 1616, that Palfrey states that the English found practically a vacant domain. In the Florida country many small tribes were so thoroughly exterminated before the coming of the whites that no trace of their existence remained except a few local names. In the interior of the continent before the French or the English had obtained a foothold, the whole country during the seventeenth century was the seat of intertribal wars so disastrous in their results as to destroy many large and powerful tribes.

With the coming of the white races the decrease in the number of the Indians went on rapidly. Estimates show such to have been the case with the Indians of the North Atlantic coast during the first quarter of the eighteenth century. Bradford and Winthrop bear witness to the small number of the natives, and to the further decrease of that number after the coming of the whites. An early writer on New York declares: "There is now (1670) but few Indians upon the island and those few no ways hurtful. It is to be admired how strangely they have decreased by the hand of God, since the English first settling in these parts." Oldmixon gives the number of Indian men in New York in 1708 as one thousand, "whereas there are seven or eight times as many English." According to the same authority, the number of Indians in New Jersey at the opening of the eighteenth century did not exceed two hundred.

A decreased birth-rate was not the least important cause of this decrease in numbers throughout all the tribes. Following the advent of the whites in the new world, "sterility became the rule and not the exception" where before the Indians were very prolific. The natives, bond or free, seemed to possess a peculiar susceptibility to the diseases of the whites, and a lack of ability to withstand their effects. The Indians of the Delaware River country complained that during the sixteen years after the coming of the Swedes, their number had been much diminished, presumably by small-pox. In both North and South Carolina, the Indians were much afflicted by this same disease in early colonial days, one tribe being entirely swept away, another nearly exhausted, and still others much reduced in numbers. Owing to diseases and other causes the several tribes in Carolina at the opening of the eighteenth century were small, most of them not numbering more than fifty men each. Douglass recorded that the Spanish Indians captured at St. Augustine and brought to New England, soon died of consumption.

Dean Berkeley who repeatedly visited Narragansett to examine the conditions and character of the Indians of that locality, in his sermon before the Society for the Propagation of the Gospel in Foreign Parts at its anniversary in 1731, bears witness to such destruction in the following statement: "The native Indians, who are said to have been thousands within the compass of this colony, do not at present amount to a thousand, including every age and sect; ... the English [having] contributed more to destroy their bodies by the use of strong liquors, than by any means to improve their minds or save their souls. This slow poison, jointly operating with the small-pox, and their wars, (but much more destructive than both), has consumed the Indians, not only in our colonies, but also far and wide upon our confines."

Intestine wars, often, as has been seen, fostered by the whites, resulted in great loss of numbers to the Indians, and sometimes even destroyed whole tribes. In consequence of a war between the Yoamaco Indians of Maryland and the Susquehanna, the former disappeared. In Virginia, between 1609 and 1669, spirituous liquors, the small-pox, war and a diminution of territory reduced the tribes to one-third of their original number. During the next twenty years they had become so much weakened that three of their principal tribes were able to send to a great Indian congress only four representatives, including attendants. By the end of the next century all had perished, except three or four of one tribe, ten or twelve of another, and a few women only of a third.

By 1780 all the Indian nations of the territory settled by the English in the south were either extinct or had retreated westward and had united with the neighboring Cherokee and Creeks. At this time the Catawba were so reduced that they possessed but seventy or eighty men. The Westo and Savannah were likewise reduced from many thousands to small numbers, and the Corannine tribe was practically destroyed.

Another cause which contributed in a measure to the passing of Indian slavery was the amalgamation of the red and black slaves. Since intercourse and marriage of slaves were not generally interfered with by the whites, it was natural that the slaves of the red and black races should intermingle. Since, also, the Indians were generally in the minority, as well as inferior in power of resistance, their physical characteristics gradually disappeared, while those of the negro remained.

By his very constitution, furthermore, the Indian seemed unfitted for servitude. He was highly susceptible to climatic changes, and unable to endure sustained labor. In his native condition he was accustomed at times to great tests of physical endurance, which, however, alternated with periods of rest and recuperation. Though authorities may differ as to the capacity of the Indian for civilization, the fact remains that civilization has only to a very small extent been assimilated by the red man. Taking into due consideration the treatment accorded him by the whites, the conclusion seems warranted that such lack of assimilation is due in some measure to the inability of the Indian to develop beyond the stage which he had already reached when discovered by the Europeans. Furthermore, the dominant idea of Indian life was the love of liberty. Heredity and environment coöperated to make the Indian a creature opposed to all restraint when exercised by an exterior force.

The general conclusion, therefore, so far as it can be determined by individual testimony, colonial legislative action and the comparative values of Indian and negro slaves, is that Indian slave labor within the territory under discussion was not, as a rule, satisfactory. Mason records that the captives distributed among the colonists as slaves at the close of the Pequot War "could not endure that yoke; few of them continuing any considerable time with their masters." Mayhew tells in 1690 of the tendency to run away shown by the Indian slaves of Massachusetts. Moses Marcy of Oxford, Massachusetts, had an Indian woman sold him by the general court prior to 1747. In that year he was discharged from his bond, she having "made way with herself after having tried to murder her mistress . . . run off and not heard from since." It is stated that the Indian female slaves of New England could not be taught to sew, to wash clothes, or to render any valuable domestic service; and that the Indian slaves of Rhode Island "only became efficient workmen under a stern and vigorous discipline." Sir Robert Montgomery, who advocated in 1717 the establishment of a colony south of Carolina, urged the use of indentured white servants, so that there might be "no necessity to use the dangerous help of Blackamoors or Indians."

The various laws, already discussed in another connection, and the numerous newspaper advertisements show Indian slaves to have been as much given to running away as their negro companions. In fact it seems not unlikely that they were more inclined toward trying to escape, for the possible chance of returning to their own people offered greater inducements for such an act than in the case of negroes.

Indian slaves as well as negroes were implicated in the various slave disturbances which occurred from time to time in the different colonies. Though there seems no evidence that Indians were usually more instrumental than negroes in creating these disturbances, yet their not infrequent participation in such events tended to lower the colonists' estimate of their value, and led to definite legislation seeking, by preventive measures and by decreeing severe punishments in case of conspiracies or uprisings, to avoid the danger which the colonists feared.

Legislation regarding slave conspiracies and uprisings was general throughout the English colonies from an early date. In some of these acts Indian slaves were expressly mentioned. In others they were included by implication in and other slaves. Reference will be made to only those acts which include Indian slaves by express mention. A South Carolina act of 1690 related to Indian and negro slaves striking a white person. The Spanish Indians were evidently considered especially undesirable, for an act passed in 1722 stated that "the importation of Spanish Indians, mustees, negroes and mulattoes may be of dangerous consequence." In 1703, Massachusetts passed "an act to prevent disorder in the night." The preamble reads: "whereas great disorders, insolences and burglaries are oftimes raised and committed in the night time by Indian, negro and mulatto servants and slaves. . . ." As late as 1769 Connecticut passed an act relating to any disturbance created by "any Indian, negro, or mulatto slave." The murder by an Indian man slave and a negro woman of an entire white family in Queens County, New York, led to the passage of an act, October 30, 1708, to prevent the conspiracy of Indian and negro slaves. A Philadelphia ordinance, also, of July 3, 1738, dealt with "the tumultuous meetings and other disorderly doings of the negroes, mulattoes and Indian servants and slaves within the city."

A second class of colonial laws related to Indian slaves alone and show that in certain of the colonies the inhabitants, for definite reasons, feared the presence of too many Indian slaves among them. Such were the laws passed by the northern colonies at the time of the Tuscarora War, by which they sought by means of heavy duties to prevent the importation of such dangerous slaves. The preamble of the Massachusetts act of 1713, for example, reads:

"Whereas divers conspiracies, outrages, barbarities, murders, burglaries, thefts and other notorious crimes and enormities, at sundry times, and especially of late, have been perpetuated and committed by Indian and other slaves within several of her majestie's plantations in America, being of a malicious, surley and revengeful spirit, rude and insolent in their behaviour, and very ungovernable, the over-great number and increase whereof within this province is likely to prove of pernicious and fatal consequences to her majestie's subjects and interest here unless speedily remedied, and is a discouragement to the importation of white Christian servants, this province being differently circumstanced from the plantations in the islands, and having great numbers of the Indian natives of the country within and about them, and at this time under the sorrowful effects of their rebellion and hostilities. . . ."

The Connecticut act passed in August, 1715, likewise for the purpose of checking the importation of Indians into the colony, is a transcript of the Massachusetts act and shows that the colonists considered a large Indian slave element in the population to be quite as undesirable as did the people of Massachusetts. The New Hampshire act of 1714 cited as a reason for checking the importation of Indians: "the over-great number and increase of such slaves within the province is likely to prove of fatal and pernicious consequences to her majesty's subjects and interests here unless speedily remedied." The Rhode Island act of July 5, 1715, similarly was passed to prevent the importation of Indian slaves, because "divers conspiracies, insurrections, rapes, thefts, and other execrable crimes have been lately perpetrated in this and the adjoining colonies by Indian slaves, etc."

Again, it seems not unlikely that the use of hired Indian servants may have had something to do with the passing of Indian slavery, though the influence was probably slight. Very early in the history of the northern colonies, Indians were employed for wages. The need for laborers could thus be partly met at very little cost. A Frenchman residing in Boston in 1687, records the wages of such servants who worked in the fields as "a shilling and a half a day and board which is eighteen pence."

The number of such Indians employed was generally small. As a hired laborer the Indian was no more reliable or trustworthy than as a slave. The keeping of Indians in the colonists' families was always considered to be more or less dangerous. Massachusetts, in 1631, and Virginia, in 1661, required that all persons should get special licenses before employing Indians. In 1634, Winthrop and his son did so. Winthrop himself speaks of the "Indians which are in our families" and mention of his Indian servant is found in other connections. As the colony grew stronger and the fear of the Indians passed away, other leading men of Massachusetts, such as Thomas Morton, the Reverend Mr. Pariss, Isaac Addington, secretary of the Council of Safety in 1714, and John Eliot employed such servants. The law was repealed in 1646, "there being more use of encouragement thereto than otherwise." That a similar employment of Indians existed in Plymouth is seen by the act of 1651 which shows the danger to the colony in providing such servants with firearms. The Praying Indians hired themselves to the whites. The New England whale fisheries employed hired Indians, at least from 1670 to 1680. During the publication of the New Testament in Massachusetts in 1661, and the translation of the New and Old Testaments and the Psalms into the Indian language by John Eliot in 1663, Green, the printer, was assisted in his work by an Indian apprentice. In Little Compton, Massachusetts, hired Indians were largely engaged in building stone fences. In 1659 and 1660, the people of Connecticut were employing the Mohegan Indians in agricultural labor, and the use of hired Indians is reported in the colony in 1774. By 1731 most of the Indians remaining in Narragansett were servants in families. The records also of Southampton, New York, show the employment of Indians for hire.

It was a part of the Puritan missionary scheme to win the heathen to Christianity by employing them in their homes where they might be brought into contact with the workings of the Christian religion. In this manner they hoped to bring the savages to a state preparatory to conversion. Something of the same purpose was intended by the early Virginia colonists. Hence, in 1619, their first legislative assembly ordered that every plantation should procure Indian youths by just means for this purpose. In 1774, the governor of Connecticut, in reply to various inquiries made by the home government regarding conditions in the colony, stated that there were then 1,363 Indians in the colony, and that many of them dwelt in English families. A similar statement was made in 1731 by Dean Berkeley to the Society for the Propagation of the Gospel in Foreign Parts. He declared that nearly all the native Indians of Rhode Island were at that time servants or laborers for the English.

Some of the earliest of the indentured servants used in America, moreover, were Indians. Reference has already been made to the Massachusetts law of 1700 seeking to avoid the abuse of the custom. In 1674, Plymouth passed a law providing that both Indians who lived idly and those who did not pay their debts on conviction could be handed over to those to whom they were indebted or to others as bond servants. The Southold town records mention Indian apprentices in

1678. Indentured male and female Indians existed in Salem in 1685. Similar records of Indian apprentices and indentured servants exist for Rhode Island, Connecticut, New Jersey and New York. As a rule these bond servants were young, for they were then more easily trained and were more tractable and useful.

In Virginia, in every agreement between Indian parents and whites, a covenant had to be entered into providing that the child be instructed in the Christian religion.

One of the most important causes for the passing of Indian slavery is found in the introduction of indentured white servants. Almost from the time of the earliest settlements these servants were an institution in the English colonies. Some of them were persons who entered voluntarily into temporary bond service to pay for passage to the new world. Some were prisoners of war. Others were convicts sent into exile for punishment. These white servants were so much desired by the colonists that requests were not infrequently sent to England for them. To encourage their voluntary coming, the colonial authorities sometimes offered them special inducements.

The number of such servants in the different colonies varied according to conditions in America and England. Naturally their number was greatest where their work was most needed. Whatever their condition before coming to America and whatever the reason for their coming, their productivity of labor, native intelligence and acquaintance with the customs and observances of civilization made them more desirable than Indian servants. There were forces, also, urging them to go to America, and forces in America drawing them there. So, until the development of the traffic in negroes, and their consequent greater use, the indentured white servants were for a while perhaps the leading factor in the decline of Indian slavery.

Another element that contributed greatly to the decline of Indian slavery was that furnished by negro slaves. The rapidly increasing number of negroes in each individual colony attested both the energy of trading companies and the desire of the colonies for the negro type of slave labor. Both indentured white servants and negro slaves, in fact, far outnumbered the Indian slaves. The sources from which the white servants and the negro slaves were drawn were well nigh inexhaustible, whereas the sources of Indian slavery were limited.

From these limited sources, also, the colonists drew but in a small degree. White servants and negro slaves were obtained by peaceful means, but the acquisition of Indian slaves not infrequently meant danger to the colony. Behind the indentured white servants and the negroes there were powerful forces supplying them to the colonists in some cases even faster than they needed them. Both indentured white servants and negroes proved more easily fitted to the life and work required of them by their masters, their labor was more productive and they were more easily controlled.

Some idea of the relative values attached to Indian and negro slaves may be obtained by a comparison of the prices for which they were sold. In Massachusetts, for instance, record exists of the sale of an Indian man slave in Newbury, in 1649, for "the quarter part of a vessel." Sewall records that on July 1, 1676, nine Indians were sold for £30. An inventory of 1690, on the other hand, appraised a single negro at £30. In the inventory of an estate in Ipswich, in 1683, "Lawrence ye Indian" was valued at £4. In the same town £5 was paid for an Indian boy and girl. The Reverend Mr. Thacher of Milton, in 1674, paid £5 down and £5 more at the end of the year for an Indian woman slave. An Indian girl brought £15 at Salem in 1710; whereas in the case of a cargo of negroes brought into Boston in 1727, as high as £80 was paid per head. In the settlement of an estate in Newbury, an Indian slave was valued at an early date at £20. In 1708, a South Carolina Indian boy was sold for £35. In 1713, a Spanish Indian boy was sold in the same town for £38. In 1725, a negro was sold in Newbury for £100, and three other negroes were valued at £132 6s. 8d. in colonial currency. In 1708, an Indian was sold at Salem for £32. An Indian girl was sold in the same town in 1710 for £15. A negro was appraised in the same town at £40. In 1764, a negro woman was sold for £8 13s. 4d. In Byfield a negro was listed in the inventory of an estate in 1689 at £60. A negro given to Cotton Mather in 1706 was purchased at an expense of £40 or £50. An Indian boy was valued in Boston in 1721 at £20, and an Indian girl at £10.

In Rhode Island the prices of Indian slaves were lower than those already mentioned, for here the Indians were sold into slavery for limited periods only. The average price at which Indians "great and small" were sold in the colony, was about thirty-two shillings.

Some of the lot brought into Rhode Island at the close of King Philip's War sold for twelve bushels of Indian corn, some for £2 10s. in silver, some for 100 pounds of wool, one for three fat sheep, two for twenty-two bushels of Indian corn. One sold in 1677 at Portsmouth for £4 10s. Indian slaves appear among other effects in the probate inventories. They were appraised at £8 and £10 each, while negroes were valued at from £60 to £80, with an average price of £50 for an able negro man and £40 for a woman. That is, a negro laborer was reckoned as the equivalent of five or six Indians. In 1718, three Indian children were worth £23. An inventory in 1723 valued the two years and ten months' service of an Indian girl at £5. The inventory of the estate of Gabriel Harris who died in 1684 in New London, Connecticut, contained the item: "An Indian maid servant, valued at £15." An Indian slave of Wethersfield was appraised in 1662 at £24. A negress and child belonging to the same estate were at the same time appraised at £22. In Derby, Connecticut, an Indian woman, twenty-six years old, sold in 1722 for £60.

The inventory of a New Jersey estate, in 1714, included an Indian man valued at £11 5s. In another inventory, in 1725, an Indian woman was valued at £30. In 1711, an Indian woman and two children were valued at £100. Similar inventories valued an Indian girl in 1696 at £30; an Indian woman in 1724 at £30; an Indian boy in 1711 at £40; . . . two Indian slaves in 1726 at £80; and two Indian slaves in 1730 at £50.

The account book of the executor of Thomas Smallcomb of York County, Virginia, 1646, contains the following items: "By two Indians sold by Sir William Berkeley, 600 lbs. By two Indians sold by Sir John Hammon, 500 lbs. By two Indians sold by Captain Thomas Petters, 600 lbs." In the records of Surrey County, 1659, occurs the following deed: "Know all men by these presents, that I, King of Waineoakes, do firmly bargaine and make sale unto Eliz. Short, her heires, executors or Assignes a boy of my nacon, named Weetoppen, from the day and date herself untill the full terme of his life, in consideracon whereof I, the said Elizabeth Short, doth for myself, my heires, executors or Assignes ingage to deliver and make sale unto the above said kinge a younge horse foale, aged one yeare, in full satisfacon for above said boy to enjoy for her pper use forever. In witness thereof, wee ye above specified, have set our hands."

The inventory of a North Carolina estate in 1693 valued a negro and his wife at £40, an Indian woman and her child at £15, and an Indian boy at £12. A bill of sale, March 5, 1711, shows an Indian between twenty and thirty-five years of age sold for £14. In 1713, the council of North Carolina decreed that "King Blount" might have eight Indians to ship to the West Indies at £10 per head. The average price for the Indian captives taken in the Tuscarora War and sold as slaves to the islands and the northern colonies appears to have been about £10 each.

A South Carolina law of 1719 states that an Indian slave was of much less value than a negro. The English of South Carolina, according to the French, were accustomed to pay (1714) the Indians fifteen pistoles for an Indian slave, while the French were able to purchase them for 115 livres. The English sold these slaves ordinarily for 300 or 400 livres.

A comparison of these prices paid for Indian slaves shows much variation at different times and places. In New England after the Indian wars the prices were low, for the chief object of the government was to get rid of the captives. In localities where the Indian's labor was in greater demand the prices rose and appear to have been highest among the English of the southern colonies. When compared with sums paid for negroes at the same time and place, the prices of Indian slaves are found to have been considerably lower. In general the prices of slaves increased during the years preceding the Revolution, but the values of Indian slaves did not equal those of negro slaves.

During the existence of Indian slavery, furthermore, there was never any general expression of opinion regarding it either in England or America, nor are there many records of opinions expressed during the colonial period as to the right or wrong of enslaving the natives. The English colonists followed the Spanish custom of reducing the Indians to a condition of slavery, but neither the English colonists nor the English government heeded the example of the later policy of the Spanish government in looking upon Indian slavery as unjust and declaring it illegal.

That personal opinions favorable or unfavorable to the enslavement of Indians were not more generally expressed is not altogether strange. The enslavement was not premeditated nor did it spring into sudden existence throughout the English colonies, but began here and there in various colonies at various times and for various reasons. The custom of enslavement came from the necessity of disposing of war captives, from the greed of traders and from the demand for labor. Individuals in the colonies, such officials of high rank and church leaders, who would naturally be expected to express an opinion either for or against the custom, themselves held Indian slaves quite as a matter of course, and found no necessity for discussing their action. Nor did the possession and employment of Indian slaves ever become sufficiently extensive to present any of the problems which later attracted the attention of the people and led to the opposition which overthrew negro slavery in several of the colonies, and incidentally, Indian slavery as well.

Yet throughout the history of Indian slavery certain expressions of opposition to the system, usually mild in nature, occurred from time to time. In the English colonies there was never any such earnest opponent to Indian slavery as the Spaniard, Las Casas, who argued directly against the enslavement of Indians from the standpoint of the injustice of reducing the natives to such a condition. Most of the opposition expressed in the English colonies was aimed at some specific instance of harsh treatment or cruel punishment of which enslavement was an incident; or it arose during the later colonial period as a part of the antagonism to slavery in general; or, as was the case in South Carolina, it revealed the attitude of one faction of the government toward the actions of another faction, and was not at all concerned in abolishing the practice of enslaving Indians as such.

The system adopted by Rhode Island at the time of King Philip's War of using the captive Indians as involuntary indentured servants for short periods of years, was anticipated by the query expressed by Roger Williams in his letter to Governor Winthrop, September 18, 1637, as to whether the captive Indians whose lives were spared should not be retained in involuntary servitude for short periods of time and then be released. This spirit of opposition to the enslavement of Indian captives for life, shown by Rhode Island during both the Pequot and King Philip wars, was somewhat out of harmony with the spirit of the times. But it should be noted that this opposition was not the expression of the entire colony. During the Pequot War it represented the feeling of the Liberal Party against the enslavement of the captive Indians, and during King Philip's War it resulted from the dominating influence of the Quaker element in the government.

The opposition of John Eliot to the enslavement of Indians during King Philip's War was similar to that shown by Roger Williams during the Pequot War, though perhaps it was prompted by a more nearly unselfish and humanitarian motive. Throughout the war Eliot remonstrated strongly against selling the captive Indians into slavery. In a letter, June 13, 1675, to the governor and council at Boston, he stated his reasons for opposing the enslavement of the captives. He first urged a politic reason: that such enslavement was likely to prolong the war and bring still further disaster upon the land by rousing the Indians to renewed hostilities. He then emphasized the Christian attitude of mercy by asserting that it is the design of Christ "not to extirpate nations but to Gospelize them." "To sell souls for money," he continued, "seems to me a dangerous merchandise. To sell them away from all means of grace, when Christ has provided means of grace for them, is the way for us to be active in the destroying of their Souls." His plea for mercy was strengthened, also, by calling attention to the letters patent of the king which urged the Indians' conversion rather than their destruction.

Some faint opposition to the enslavement of Indians was expressed by Samuel Sewall of Massachusetts in 1706, called forth by an act passed by Massachusetts against Indians and negroes. Perhaps something was accomplished by the protest, though the act either failed to pass or was repealed, since no trace of it remains.

In 1729, Ralph Sandiford published a work entitled: "The Mystery of Iniquity in a Brief Examination of the Practice of the Times." In the dedication of his book, he speaks of going to South Carolina, and of refusing the bounty of a rich colonist there because his riches had been obtained through the labor of negro and Indian slaves. He declares that negroes and Indians who are the Lord's freemen cannot be slaves to Christians. He further asserts that the matter he is aiming at is "this trading in mankind, which is pernicious to the Publick, but more especially to the common-wealth of Israel; which raised forth a zeal in Men for the House of the Lord, which would have even consumed men had not I witnessed against this rottenness and hypocrisy that would introduce itself amongst the saints, whereby, as way-marks, they lead many into the same corrupt practice which is contrary to the Principal of Truth, which is over the Heads of such Transgressors, that the Righteous in all Churches are undefiled with it, for their Bodies are the Temples of the Holy Ghost to dwell in, which they cannot defile with Babylon, who is Harloted from the Truth to feed upon the Flesh or receive nourishment from the blood of the poor Negro or Indian captive, or whomsoever ravenous Nature (which is the Beast's work) has power to prey upon."

Granville Sharp, in 1767, published in London a protest against slavery, in which he declared there could be no reasonable pretense for holding either negroes or Indians in slavery. In discussing the bringing about of a state of slavery through contract he declared that "in such a case there would still remain a great suspicion that some undue advantage had been taken of the Indians' ignorance concerning the nature of such a bond." Slavery he declared a "shameless prostitution and infringement on the common and natural rights of mankind." Every inhabitant of the king's realm, regardless of color, he declared to be the king's subject, and asserted that no one, therefore, had a moral or legal right to enslave any such subject. If color were a basis for slavery, he argued, then in a short time any Englishman might be enslaved since there was but little difference between the complexion of a northern Indian and a white man.

Anthony Benezet, about 1750, began to express his opposition to slavery in the almanacs and newspapers of the day. After three separate publications dealing with slavery in general, he issued in 1784 a book entitled "Some Observations on the Situation, Disposition and Character of the Indian Natives of this Continent." In this he refers to the kindness, hospitality and generosity of the Indians toward the English in the early days of trade, and laments the fact that "the adventurers from a thirst of gain overreached the natives" so that the latter "saw some of their friends and relatives treacherously entrapped and carried away to be sold as slaves."

Throughout the colonial period the Society of Friends showed more or less opposition to slavery, although the members of the Society held slaves. From 1688 a certain amount of agitation concerning the matter is apparent in the records of the various quarterly and yearly meetings in Pennsylvania and the Jerseys. In the records of the Philadelphia Yearly Meeting for the year 1719, is found the first mention of Indian slaves made in the minutes of the Yearly Meeting. In that year, after an earnest admonition to Friends to refrain from selling, trading or exchanging in any way any spirituous liquors with the Indians, the Yearly Meeting voted: "And to avoid giving them occasion of discontent, it is desired, that Friends do not buy or sell Indian slaves." From the wording of the record it may be concluded that the basis for the Friends' action was not the idea of any moral wrongdoing attached to the enslavement of Indians, but rather the possible harm that might come to the colony through the discontent which enslavement might cause among the free Indians. And, judging from the previous action of the Society taken with regard to slavery, it may also be concluded that this basis for the opposition to the trade in Indian slaves was used as a means of calling the immediate attention of its members to the matter, and that the reason for the opposition of the Meeting to trading in Indians was the same as that to negro slavery: "caution not censure."

Some criticism was expressed in Massachusetts at the seizure of the Indians at Cocheco in 1676, and the subsequent transportation of part of the number captured by order of the government. Such criticism, however, was not aimed at the action of the government in selling the Indians as slaves, but at the breach of faith in seizing Indians at peace.

In South Carolina, as already observed, the proprietors sanctioned enslavement of Indians when carried on for their own financial benefit, and opposed it when carried on by the colonial authorities. The colonial officials favored the practice and carried it on both as a means of meeting colonial expenses and as a source of personal income. In this respect the action of the existing colonial government of South Carolina differs materially from that of the officials of any other colony. Nowhere else was the desire for personal gain a controlling cause for the disposal of captives taken in war and hence colonial property.

In contrast to these incidental expressions of personal opposition to the enslavement of Indians, stands the ownership and employment of them by leading colonists. The New Englanders not only bought Indians at the time of the Indian wars, but also sent requests to the colonial officials for them. Captain Stoughton wrote to Governor Winthrop from the scene of the Swamp Fight: "By this pinnace, you shall receive 48 or 50 women and children, unless there stay any here to be helpful, concerning which there is one, I formerly mentioned, that is the *fairest* and *largest* amongst them to whom I have given a coate to cloathe her. It is my desire to have her for a servant, if it may stand to your good liking, else not. There is a little squaw that steward Culacut desireth, to whom he hath given a coate. Lieut. Davenport also desireth one, to wit, a small one, that has three strokes upon her stomach. . . . He desireth her, if it will stand with your good liking. Sosomon, the Indian, desireth a young little squaw, which , I know not."

The Reverend Hugh Peter also wrote to Governor Winthrop in 1637: "Mr. Endecot and my selfe salute you in the Lord Jesus, etc. Wee haue heard of a diuidence of women and children in the bay and would bee glad of a share viz: a young woman or girle and a boy if you thinke good: I wrote to you for some boyes for Bermudas, which I thinke is considerable." In July, 1637, Roger Williams petitioned Governor Winthrop for an Indian as follows: "It having againe pleased the Most High to put into your hands another miserable droue of Adams degenerate seede, & our brethren by nature, I am bold (if I may not offend in it) to request the keeping & bringing vp of one of the children. I haue fixed mine eye on this litle one with the red about his neck, but I will not be peremptory in my choice, but will rest in your loving pleasure for him or any, &c."

The barrister, Emanuel Downing, writing to John Winthrop in 1645, clearly illustrates the view of his day. He says: "A warr with the Narraganset is verie considerable to this plantation, ffor I doubt whither yt be not synne in vs, hauing power in our hands, to suffer them to maynteyne the worship of the devill which their paw waves often doe; 21ie, If vpon a Just warre the Lord should deliuer them into our hands, wee might easily haue men woemen and children enough to exchange for Moores, which wilbe more gaynefull pilladge for vs then wee conceive, for I doe not see how wee can thrive vntill wee gett(...) into a stock of slaves sufficient to doe all our buisines, for our children's children will hardly see this great Continent filled with people, soe that our servants will still desire freedome to plant for them selues, and not stay but for verie great wages. And I suppose you know verie well how wee shall maynteyne 20 Moores cheaper then one Englishe servant."

In only a few of the English-American colonies were attempts made by legislative enactment to end Indian slavery as a system separate from negro slavery. The reasons for this fact are obvious. In the course of time Indian slavery became absorbed by the institution of negro slavery to such an extent that it attracted no attention. With the various colonial acts at the time of the Tuscarora War, which forbade the further importation of Indians into the northern colonies, the system was maintained only by the natural increase of the Indian slaves already in existence. So Indian slavery existed as an unimportant system along with and overshadowed by negro slavery until the spirit of opposition to the institution of slavery in general grew sufficiently strong to lead to legislation providing for the abolition of slavery in various colonies.

The first colony to take such legislative action was Virginia, but in this instance there is a slight possibility that the intent of the act to be discussed was quite different from what later interpretations have considered it to be. In 1691, "by implication rather than by the terms of the act" Indian slavery was rendered illegal by an act authorizing a free and open trade for all persons, at all times and all places, with all Indians whatsoever. It is barely possible that the legislature may have viewed the act as a treaty with a nation which, *ipso facto,* was recognized as of equal status as to freedom, while the treaty in no wise prevented subsequent enslavement of individuals sold by the nation itself to the whites, or of hostile captives, or of Indians not native North Americans as generally understood. But it is generally considered that the act was intended, as it was later construed, to acknowledge the free condition of all Indians. If the colonists of the time so construed it, they intentionally disobeyed it and enslavement of Indians continued. In 1705, a similar act was passed with the same enacting clause. Cases arising later showed a similar failure to accomplish desired results.

In 1777, the assembly, when called to pass upon the matter, decided that no Indians brought into Virginia since the passage of the act of 1705, or their descendants, could be slaves in the commonwealth. At that time knowledge of the existence of the act of 1691 seems to have disappeared. Even after the decision of the assembly in 1777, the settlement of the matter was so far uncertain as to give rise to certain cases in law in 1792 and 1793, appealed from the County Court to the Court of Appeals to maintain the right to the services of the descendants of Indians enslaved after the passing of the act of 1705. In both these cases the higher court affirmed the decision of the lower courts which granted freedom to the Indians thus held as slaves, and which interpreted the act of 1705 as repealing all former acts permitting the existence of Indian slavery in the colony.

In 1806, the Supreme Court of the state decided that Indians had always been considered free persons in fact and in right, and that the presumption was that all Indians introduced into the state at any time, were *prima facie* presumed to be free, or that, if the date of their introduction did not appear, the *prima facie* presumption was that they were American Indians, or brought in after the act of 1705, and therefore free. In 1808, came the judicial recognition of the law of 1691. A Supreme Court decision of that year declared "that no native American Indian brought into Virginia since the year 1691 could under any circumstances lawfully be made a slave." It was also held by the court that if a female ancestor of a person asserting a right to freedom, whose genealogy could be traced back to such ancestor by females only, be proved to have been an Indian, "it seems incumbent on those who claim such person as a slave to show that such ancestor, or some female from which she descended, was brought into Virginia between the years 1679 and 1691, and under circumstances which, according to the laws then in force, created a right to hold her in slavery."

In the case of Butt v. Rachel *et al.,* 1814, the plaintiffs claimed their freedom as descendants of a native female Indian who was brought into Virginia about the year 1747. The court instructed the jury that no native American Indian brought into Virginia since the year 1691, could, under any circumstances, be made a slave. The defendant claimed to hold the slaves on the ground that they were the descendants of a native American Indian woman who was held as a slave on the island of Jamaica, and brought to Virginia as a slave about the year 1747. The defendant moved the court to instruct the jury that a native American Indian held as a slave on the island of Jamaica by the laws of that island, might be held as a slave when imported into Virginia. The court refused so to do, and judgment was awarded the plaintiff. The case was appealed, but the court sustained the judgment.

Considering the possibility already mentioned that the act of 1691 may have been intended to apply only to Indians outside the colony and that it did not apply to those in the colony, either free or enslaved, and the fact that the later legislative action of 1777 and the cases in law already mentioned show that the law was either misconstrued or ignored, the acts of 1691 and 1705, so far as putting an end to Indian slavery in Virginia in colonial times is concerned, might as well have never existed.

At a later date, South Carolina also enacted laws which by court decision, were interpreted to mean the abolition of Indian slavery. The act of 1740 stated that "all negroes, Indians (free Indians in amity with this government, and negroes, mulattoes, or mestizoes who are now free, excepted), mulattoes, or mestizoes, who are now or who shall hereafter be in this province, and all their issue and offspring born, or to be born, shall be, and they are hereby declared to be and remain forever hereafter, absolute slaves, and shall follow the condition of the mother." Under this provision it has been uniformly held that color was *prima facie* evidence that the party bearing the color of a negro, mulatto or mestizo, was a slave; but the same *prima facie* result did not follow from the Indian color, according to the decision of the courts. After the passage of the act, Indians and descendants of Indians were regarded as free Indians in amity with the government, until the contrary was shown. Elsewhere in the act of 1740 it is declared that "every negro, Indian, mulatto, and mestizo is a slave unless the contrary can be made to appear" yet in the same act it is immediately thereafter provided—"the Indians in amity with this government excepted, in which case the burden of the proof shall lie on the defendant" that is on the person claiming the Indian plaintiff to be a slave. This latter clause of the provision grew to be considered the rule, and so the race of slave Indians, or of Indians not in amity with the government, passed out of existence and the previous part of the provision lost its application.

By an act of May 18, 1652, passed by the Commissioners of Providence Plantations and Warwick, it was provided that "no black mankind, or white, being forced to covenant, bond or otherwise, serve any man or his assigns longer than ten years, or until they come to be twenty-four years of age, if they be taken under fourteen, from the time of their coming within the limits of this colony, and at the end or term of ten years to set them free, as the matter is with the English servants." The act makes no mention of Indian slaves, doubtless because at this early date there were not enough in the colony to arouse interest in their condition.

When at the time of King Philip's War Indian slaves were being transported by Massachusetts and distributed among the settlements, Rhode Island, March, 1676, passed a law concerning them similar to the law of 1652 relating to negroes. This act provided that "no Indian in this colony be a slave but only to pay their debts, or for their bringing up, or courtesy they have received, or to perform covenant, as if they had been countrymen not in war."

In colonial New York it was customary to discriminate between the free natives of the colony and those brought from the Spanish West Indies. On December 5, 1679, it was voted at a council meeting that "all Indians here are free and not slaves, except such as have been formerly brought from the Bay of Campeachy and other foreign parts" some of whom were slaves in the colony. Concerning such foreign Indians the act provided: "But if any shall be brought hereafter within the space of six months, they are to be disposed of as soon as may be, out of the government, but after the expiration of six months, all that shall be brought here from these parts shall be free." On April 20, 1680, a decree of governor and council repeated this resolution as a formal order. Apparently no immediate attention was given to the enforcement of the law. Later some action regarding the matter was taken when the council, October 11, 1687, ordered that certain Spanish Indians brought from the Bay of Campeachy and sold as slaves in the colony should be set free. On July 30, 1688, the council again took up the question of foreign Indians. It was resolved "that all Indian slaves within this province subject to the King of Spain, that can give an account of their Christian faith and say the Lord's Prayer, be forthwith set at liberty, and sent home by the first conveyance, and likewise them that shall hereafter come to the province." On the same day the council rejected a petition of the owner to retain in the colony an Indian slave purchased outside the colony and brought to New York.

The numerous petitions to the governor to free such Indians from slavery, and his attitude in the matter, show the colonial authorities willing to stand by their legislation on the subject. On December 28, 1700, such a petition was presented by the mayor and aldermen of New York City to the governor, demanding the release of a free born Indian woman, a native of Curaçao, then held as a slave in New York. On July 15, 1703, Jacobus Kierstead, a mariner, of New York, petitioned the governor regarding an Indian brought by him from the West Indies and sold as a slave. Soon after Governor Hunter's arrival in the province a petition was handed him on behalf of a number of free-born Spanish subjects thus held as slaves. Among the victims was one Stephen Domingo, a native of Carthagena, who had been held as a slave for eight years. Hunter became interested in the matter and wrote to the Board of Trade, June 23, 1712, that there were Spanish Indians in New York who had been unjustly kept there in slavery for many years. He discovered that one Husea and one John, both held as slaves and both engaged in the slave conspiracy of 1712, were brought to New York as prisoners of war taken from a Spanish vessel by a privateer; that they were SpanishAmerican Indians and subjects of the king of Spain, sold as slaves in New York and kept in bondage six or seven years "by reason of their color which is swarthy." They declared they were sold among many others of the same color and the same country. These two Indians Governor Hunter reprieved awaiting the queen's pleasure. The Indians who petitioned, though he "secretly pitied their condition" he was unable to help as he had no other evidence than their words.

Rhode Island is the only other colony which took direct action concerning Spanish Indians, but even Rhode Island never put forth any general legislation on the matter. Special action was taken similar to that in New York. In 1746, the general assembly of Rhode Island and Providence Plantations voted to send back to the West Indies certain free subjects of the king of Spain who had been captured and sold in the colony as slaves. These, like the others mentioned, were captives taken in the recent war with Spain. Here, as in New York, the point involved was one of international importance, and the Indians concerned were considered, not as Indians but as the objects about which the point was raised.

The other colonies of the original thirteen which finally took legislative action to end the institution of slavery in general did not accomplish such action during the colonial period; so the conclusion remains that with the exception of Virginia, South Carolina, Rhode Island and New York, none of the colonies ever declared Indian slavery illegal.